William Cottringer

You Can HAVE YOUR CHEESE and Eat It Too

Closing the Gap Between Where You Are and Where You Want to Be

For permission requests, contact the publisher at:

Executive Excellence Publishing
1366 East 1120 South
Provo, UT 84606
Phone: 1-801-375-4060
Toll Free: 1-800-304-9782
Fax: 1-801-377-5960
www.eep.com

For Executive Excellence books, magazines and other products, contact Executive Excellence directly. Call 1-800-304-9782, fax 1-801-377-5960, or visit our website at www.eep.com.

Printed in the United States

Printed by Bang Printing

10 9 8 7 6 5 4 3 2 1

Library of Congress Cataloging-in-Publication Data

Cottringer, William, 1944-
You can have your cheese and eat it too : closing the gap between where you are and where you want to be / William Cottringer.
p. cm.
ISBN 1-930771-14-2
1. Conduct of life--Miscellanea. I. Title.
BF637.C5 C68 2001
658--dc21

2001005313

Advance Praise for *You Can Have Your Cheese and Eat It Too*

"This powerful, practical book cuts right to the heart of what it takes to live with greater balance and achieve more than ever before."
—Brian Tracy, author of *Success Is a Journey* and *The 100 Absolutely Unbreakable Laws of Business Success*

"*You Can Have Your Cheese and Eat It Too* is all about the cat-and-mouse conspiracy that sometimes makes life a battle between chaos and order. Enjoy and use this practical 'theory of life.' "
—Ken Blanchard, Coauthor of *The One Minute Manager*

"*You Can Have Your Cheese and Eat It Too* provides an insightful and practical look at how to bring greater harmony and happiness to your life easily and simply. This book is a must-read for people who are passionate about having their cheese and eating it too!"
—Richard Chang, CEO, Richard Chang Associates, Inc. and author of *The Passion Plan*

"Bill Cottringer's book is a treasure. His message is compelling—getting what you want, while living a life of integrity. His style is delightful, tapping the reader's impulse to turn one more page."
—Allen Johnson, Ph.D., president, Johnson Dynamics and author of *The Power Within*

"Thank you, Dr. Cottringer, for providing an avalanche of insight, humor, and gentle guidance that, if applied, will guarantee that our daily acts of working, loving, and living are more productive and fulfilling."
—Dr. Laurie Anderson, psychologist, organizational consultant, executive coach, and author

"*You Can Have Your Cheese and Eat It Too* provides delightful insight into our self-made chaotic world of complexity and simplicity, perplexity and clarity. Laugh and learn through this tale full of illusion, confusion, and amusion."
—Karyn Buxman, President, HUMORx

"This book offers an amazingly clear explanation of how we get sidetracked with chaos and confusion and then a blueprint for getting back on the right path to restore order to our lives."
—Maurie Rayner, CEO Corporate-Recharge and legendary Australian water sports coach

"Some timeless life principles presented in a clever and unconventional story line. An interesting presentation of what it takes to achieve a more fulfilling, accepting, and balanced life."

—Kevin and Jackie Freiberg, authors of NUTS!

"Bill Cottringer's remarkable book shows how in the 'first half' of our lives we unthinkingly spread chaos and confusion with the illusion that certain 'truths' about our unique perception of reality are more true and correct at the expense of others being declared 'false.' Then, during the 'second half' of our lives, we start restoring order through simple recognition of the underlying unity of all things."

—Mark Watts, CEO Electronic University

"The bottom line in any business is closing the gap between where you are and where you want to be. This book offers many valuable and practical ways to do that for both personal and business development. An easy and enjoyable book to read."

—Eugene Buss, Vice President, Burns/Pinkerton Security Services

"Read this book! Dr. Cottringer has outlined practical activities which will help you live life more meaningfully. Using delightful storytelling, he creatively reminds us of the power of the human spirit."

—Michael Vandermark, Ph.D., Director of Corporate Programs, Chopra Center for Well-being

"Cottringer has given us a rare treasure—deep wisdom conveyed through a very unique and engaging story. This book is positive, smart, funny, challenging, and important. Read this book. You'll want to send Dr. Cottringer a warm thank you note when you are done."

—Bruce Tulgan, author of *WINNING THE TALENT WARS*

"Don't miss the book's priceless success formula: Dream big, be clever, use your talent fully, be reverent with everything, work hard, and never quit."

—Sean Smith, Hollywood Actor.

"A unique, fun, and easy-to-read book that will help you make it a winning life, faster!"

—Wolf J. Rinke, PhD, author of *Make It a Winning Life*

"This book is a great discovery to breaking down the chaos in our lives and finding our own joy and harmony."

—Sarah Fitz-Gerald, #1 Ranked Women's Squash Player

Acknowledgments

Over the past 30 years, many people have influenced the background thinking and writing of this book. I apologize if any of them are overlooked in the brief list of acknowledgments. Specifically, I would like to thank the following people:

My Mom and Dad, Bill and Edythe, who brought me up in a physically comfortable, physiologically healthy and spiritually sound environment.

Prolific authors Alan Watts, Jack Canfield, Ken Blanchard, and Stephen Covey, who all got me thinking about the most important things.

Professor Clinton Meek at Southern Illinois University, who expanded my mind by guiding me to read most of the interesting books in the "Suggested Reading" list.

My first secretary at the Omaha Correctional Center, Trina Carroll, who typed the first 14-page mini-version of this story as *Bridging the Gap*.

My second secretary there, Joyce Kudrna, who unknowingly challenged me to solve the riddle of how to have my cheese and eat it too.

The warden there, Karen Shortridge, who demonstrated how to ask more questions to get better answers and emphasized the importance of maintaining ideals.

My silent jokester mentor, Professor Herb Gross, who planted the seed of my "P" Point concept of the critical little things that get big results.

My high-school buddy, Al DeMartini, who recently lost his younger brother in the New York terrorist attack. Frank was the construction manager of the World Trade Center and gave his life in helping others to safety.

My two life-long friends, Bob Wohlgemuth and Larry Kelly, who both encouraged my writing, read everything I ever wrote, and supported me in my darkest hour.

My oldest daughter, Deisha, who has always known how to have her cheese and eat it too and showed me how by giving me a second chance to be a good dad.

My youngest daughter, Abigail, in hopes that she will continue to follow her dream and learn how to focus on what she needs to do to achieve it. I hope this book helps.

My sweet granddaughter, Hannah, who has a simple approach to life—laugh when it is right and yell when it is not.

My true love, Kathy Haberer (Toots), who gave me more cheese than she'll ever know and whose love is right up there behind God's. Her mom and dad deserve some credit too for raising such a great daughter.

My dear Aussie mate, Maurie Rayner, who is now deceased. He helped me get physically fit, and I helped him get mentally fit. We were a great team.

My long-time soul mate, Melinda Roedemeier, who is also now deceased. She taught me how to be friends after being lovers. I'd like to dedicate this book to both her and Maurie.

My present and best-ever employers, Tom, John, and James Boldt, who graciously allowed me to occasionally sneak in work time to tweak cheese flavors, colors, and textures. They also supported my training ideas from the book.

Father James Harris whose role modeling of the virtues of inclusion is the best I've ever seen. We say many of the same things in slightly different languages.

Spencer Johnson, MD, whose bestseller, *Who Moved My Cheese?* partially stimulated my idea of the cat-and-mouse conspiracy.

Ken Shelton, Nathan Lyon, Courtney Hammond, and Mark Jessen at Executive Excellence Publishing, who recognized raw cheese and helped turn it into properly-aged Swiss.

Contents

Preface

Tell me quick and tell me true or else my friend, the heck with you. Less of how your product came to be, and more of what it does for me.
—impatient mouse

We are all on a journey. We try to fit in with our surroundings and improve what we are fitting into. We are continually trying to close the gap between where we are and where we want to be. The trouble is we are often impatient and try to make improvements and close the gap before we even understand what we are trying to fit into or what the gap is all about. And so we create much chaos before we finally reach the simplicity on the other side of complexity. Our destination is our Prosperity Zone where we can see most clearly how to close the gap and be where we want to be. This book is a summary of my own journey.

I have written this book for three main reasons. The first one is selfish, the second unselfish, and the third, just fun:

First, to reach closure in my journey by clarifying my own chaos and restoring the order necessary to get where I want to be.

Second, to offer some chaos-clarifying and order-restoring clues for others who are still trying to get to the simplicity just on the other side of their complexity.

Third, to amuse others who have already arrived here ahead of me, by sharing the details of my particular landing spot.

Long ago, I started with a basic assumption that we all really do know how to have our "cheese" and eat it too. We occasionally forget this ability and need some periodic friendly reminders of how to be our best and get to where we want to be. In my lifetime, I have verified this assumption, and the results of my efforts are this book.

This book has undergone a complete metamorphosis. The main ideas started popping into my head nearly 30 years ago. These ideas were in the form of various mental mistakes that we all make trying to get where we want to be. The first printed version was a 14-page booklet for prison inmates entitled, *Bridging Your Own Gap*. Their gap was going from prison to the free world.

During the in-between time, this little book has gradually evolved into three books: *Rebraining for 2000*, *Getting It*, and *Passwords to The Prosperity Zone*. The ideas and material in these books were developed through several different careers in law enforcement, corrections, mental health, college teaching, private security, building maintenance, and business consulting. Over the years my "audience" has grown through the ranks of mental patients, prison inmates, college students, security guards, janitors, managers, and now, finally, everybody.

Despite many years of perseverance in trying to get these manuscripts published, the best I could do was to print them for friends and for self-consumption. I had a dream of writing a book, worked hard to make the dream come true, but nothing happened. I knew that the information was important and useful because several parts of these books had already been published in magazines; apparently somebody thought they were worth reading.

At this point the manuscript contained serious flaws I didn't want to acknowledge. I had written and re-written the words more times than I want to remember, but I was only changing the words, not the nature of the ideas or the style in which they were packaged. The original formats were too stiff, and the ideas weren't presented cleverly enough to compete for bookshelf space. Plus, a proper title that communicated everything with clarity, creativity, and unity, was still out there somewhere. Loose ends, more work.

Then some radical changes occurred. My domestic partner, Toots, and I adopted two little Siamese kittens. This was odd because she had always been petless, and I was always a dog person. After re-reading all my words, glancing through *Who Moved My Cheese?*, reading a few popular spiritual books, and watching these kittens play, I had a better idea. I translated all my ideas into a simple, clever story about a cat-and-mouse conspiracy ingeniously designed to make life more interesting and challenging. The cat-and-mouse conspiracy is a metaphor for my idea that people keep themselves from getting to where they want to be by creating unnecessary chaos, but they conveniently forget that fact, along with the order-restoring solutions for closing their gap.

I finally got smart and sent this new manuscript with the other three, to an editor who had already published a few of my articles. The playful writing and fonts caught their attention, and soon we had a business arrangement. We just weren't sure in which direction we were moving.

After finishing this first cat-and-mouse story, I later wrote an addition in which the two cat heroes raise their own kittens and want to pass on all the wisdom they learned from the earlier conspiracy. Finally I merged these two playful stories into this book—Part I: The Problem and Part II: The Solution.

The Problem is the gap between where we are and where we want to be and the various mental mousetraps, such as instantaneousmania, either-oring and duncery, in which we get caught while trying to close this gap. The Solution is to understand the gap better and then close it by applying "P" Points, or little things that get big results in avoiding these mental mousetraps; following some sensible Do's and Don'ts; and answering important questions, such as Who am I? and Where am I going?

Together, this prescription solves the most important riddle that perplexes us all: How to have your cheese and eat it too. Finally I had a title, and my dream started coming true. Right now I am wondering just how successful this thing will be, and whether or not I am ready for it. As the saying goes, "Be careful what you want because you will likely get it, just not exactly when and how you expect it."

Be sure and read "About the Author" at the end of the book; it has more information about what influenced the ideas in this book.

Introduction

You can't lift a pebble with one finger.

—Native American saying

How can you have your cheese and eat it too? This is a taunting riddle that we often dismiss too quickly as irrelevant, nonsensical, or downright impossible. Why bother with such foolishness? However, solving this little riddle may have more to do with being successful and happy in life than you might first imagine. Solutions to this riddle are possible, and they will get you more cheese than you will probably ever need. The key is to spend more time examining the question than searching for a particular answer.

Just to make sure we all know what I mean by "cheese," let me define it simply and clearly:

Cheese is anything you think you want that you think you can get by doing certain things.

Small cheese is money, a house, a car, a job, and some degree of success—those sorts of things. Big cheese is happiness, peace of mind, self-actualization, contentment, wisdom, and enlightenment.

The simplest solution to this riddle is to have a little and eat a little, without doing either at the expense of the other. For instance, we all want the freedom of being able to express our individual uniqueness, while at the same time demanding the security of being treated fairly and equally. At first this often results in an impossible, either-or choice in which we assume that we can't have our cheese and eat it too. However, by being assertive in exercising responsible freedom with others and treating them the same way you want to be treated, you are in fact having your cheese and eating it too.

Another solution has to do with how you define having your cheese and eating it too. With your private definitions come certain expectations, which are often unmet, leaving you with no cheese at all. Being more open and flexible about exactly what having your cheese and eating it too actually means may allow you to do both. Savoring a small bite and then freezing the rest for later does just that. Taking a picture of yourself eating your cheese does both too.

Still another solution is to get priorities straight with the many either-or situations that confront you. For example, in many situations you have a choice to either rebel or obey. Being a natural rebel, you may be missing out on the grand sense of pure freedom that comes from choosing to obey, first.

We all have wants and needs, and knowing which ones to meet first can often result in having both. As another example, you need to fit into every situation and at the same time you want to improve the situation you are fitting into. Most times you get in a hurry and focus more on the second part of this equation, instead of first trying to fit in and learning what it is you are trying to change. Approaching this dilemma in the right order will help you be more effective all the way around. Reversing priorities may be the most common way to not have your cheese and eat it too.

Then, of course, there are those either-or choices that leave you between a rock and a hard place. In these situations, the choices themselves need to be questioned and replaced. Who wants to choose between a lousy marriage and a costly divorce? Divorces don't have to be costly, and marriages don't have to be lousy.

If you are having difficulty seeing these alternative solutions, you may not be in the right place to see best. Are you distracted by the nagging sense that there is a gap between where you are and where you want to be? You may want to have your cheese and eat it too, but these two objectives are too far apart to see clearly what they are and how to have them both.

The best vantage point, ironically, is somewhere in between where you are and where you want to be. This book gently reminds you of a few things you may need to stop doing altogether—and a few others you may need to start doing smarter—so you can reach this wonderful place.

To get here, you have to first understand the seven deadly mental mousetraps that keep you from seeing the problem. Once you begin seeing the problem, the solution is easy. The easiest solution to closing your gap between here and there is to shorten the distance to where you are running and, at the same time, run faster. You can do this by eliminating the Don'ts and practicing the Do's. This is the easiest and quickest way you can have your cheese and eat it too. Why not enjoy both?

A Challenge to Readers

Something has always plagued me about the business of making productive changes and becoming successful and happy. There are certainly already more than enough self-help books on the market, but in all honesty, all these books collectively still aren't making much of a dent in most ordinary peoples' lack of success and happiness. If the self-help industry were based on actual results, it would probably be out of business.

Why? For many reasons, ranging from people wanting easy and simple solutions to difficult, complex problems, to different people each needing entirely different formats for hearing what they need to hear. My challenge is to improve the chances that you can have your cheese and eat it too—that this book will actually help you do just that. I want to be sure that you put these good ideas in action to make a real difference. That is my small wish. The last thing I want is for the book to get lost on a bookshelf, collecting dust somewhere. I have worked too hard to allow that to happen.

So how can I have my own cheese and eat it too? After a few weeks of doing nothing but asking difficult questions, I came up with the way out of this dilemma. After all, I don't want to be a victim of my own cheese paradox—writing a worthwhile book and then not having you apply the information.

Three Questions

After all my thinking and conversations, I finally realized that there are three critical questions people must ask and struggle to answer before they are ready to implement the best and most useful information. Without taking time to do this, all the wisdom in the world won't stick and become a good habit. You need to remove some formidable barriers in the way of semi-conscious motivations before you are ready to accept and eventually use good information. To do this you have to ask and answer these three fundamental questions, before you are ready to start having your cheese and eating it too.

1. How do I sabotage my own success?

The fear of success is insidious. Most of this fear is based on some major assumptions of what might happen when you become successful. A few of these assumptions include the following: What will you have to do to achieve success? What will you have to give up? What will it be like? What will you have to do to maintain success? What will happen to you if you lose it?" There are a lot more "what if" questions that cause distracting and often debilitating anxiety just below the surface.

Your mind can go fairly wild with anticipation, before you even become successful at what you are trying to do. In this sense you are preventing the smaller successes, which could lead to bigger ones, from happening.

Facing your darker side is not pleasant or easy, but you will never get anywhere until you take ultimate responsibility for where you are or where you are not. You can't begin to close the gap between where you are and where you want to be until you see who created that gap—you. Once you learn a little bit about your own worst self-sabotaging behaviors and take ownership for this passive self-destruction, you can begin to eliminate the need for such needless, unproductive behavior.

There is a second part of this first question:

Why don't I apply all the good things I learn and know?

Some day I would like to download my own brain to retrieve all the fabulous learning that has passed through it. For nearly 40 years I have been taught, guided, and motivated by the best of the best from the cliffs of Big Sur to the red rocks of the Australian outback. But I am the first to ask, why did so much of that good stuff not take? Why do we learn so many good things and then not apply them? If I had applied one-tenth of the things I knew were right and good, I would have blissfully dissolved in nirvana by now.

We all have to come to grips with the question of why we keep pushing the cheese away. My own answer to this nagging question seems to be my insatiable need to avoid boredom and stir up new excitement. I always need a new challenge. Being able to do something well is anti-climactic.

In the end, you have to look yourself in the mirror and ask this question and keep asking it until you get your answer. It may be later than you think, so what are you waiting for?

Here is another thought: Maybe we sabotage ourselves by trying to control too much. We need to focus more on trying to control the controllable and relevant things. For example we can control our interpretations of things that happen to us and our reactions to those interpretations. Once we learn how to control these interpretations and reactions, we can gradually try to expand our influence to other things.

The fact is, we can only influence reality to the degree we fully understand the interconnections of things behind the scenes.

2. For whom (or what) am I doing all this?

It usually takes a very long time to understand why you are or aren't doing something, and then even longer to do anything about it. The trouble is, you often try to do the right things for the wrong person or the wrong reasons.

Long ago I learned that you can't make another person happy, only unhappy. But that still didn't keep me from franticly trying to achieve things in order to please or impress someone else. However, the sense of satisfaction and accomplishment never seems to come to you when you are doing something for someone else for the wrong reason.

We are often hesitant to do something for ourselves because we don't want to be selfish. Sooner or later we have to shed that guilt. You can only do something you want to do because it is right to do for yourself. Doing it for others or for ulterior reasons is not the way to go. It will never work out in your favor. You expect certain results, and when you don't get them you become disappointed and frustrated, decreasing your confidence, chances for success, and happiness.

3. What is the best I am capable of?

Many of us dream of greatness but only a few take the first step to develop a detailed plan to get there. Even fewer of us endure the difficult voyage that is required to make our dreams come true. We perceive ourselves in a catch-22 position, which is part of the reason for our lazy mediocrity.

On the one hand we are teased into believing we can do anything we put our mind to. On the other hand there are subtle warnings everywhere that tell us not to set our goals too high so we don't doom ourselves to unnecessary disappointment and failure. To be safe we often settle for far worse than second best. By that time we may have completely forgotten what we were capable of doing at the beginning.

The truth is you are capable of doing anything you think you are capable of doing. But that doesn't mean it will happen by magic or exactly the way you want it to. Your efforts have to become natural, and they have to meet the right opportunity.

Your dreams won't come true if you are not willing to be flexible with your goals and how to achieve them. Nor will they be fulfilled if you refuse to make difficult choices and sacrifices, take risky chances, and persevere long enough to make your dreams come true. You also have to be doing it all for the right person and the right reason. This is competition against your own self at its best. Only you can move the bar higher and make a better effort to get over it.

To be the best you are capable of being involves finding your single best talent and then devoting your life to developing it fully and doing it frequently. Forget about what you can't do and focus solely on what you do best and do it. Dream big, be clever and work hard.

Having the courage to ask these three critical questions and then making the effort to find answers will enable a surge of personal growth. You will accept all this good information and apply it to make a difference. You are about to learn how you can have your cheese and eat it too.

Doc

PART I

The Problem

Good propaganda must precede real events.

—retired cat military leader

This is the nearly true story of how two mischievous Siamese kittens and two older, wiser mice got together and conspired to carry out a clever plan to give life meaning and purpose and make it interesting, challenging, and fun. You see, recently a smart mouse doctor, Spencer Johnson, wrote an ingenious book that was extremely successful in helping mice adapt better to the fast-changing world. His best-selling book, *Who Moved My Cheese?* made things too easy for the mice and too difficult for the cats. Obviously something had to be done to correct this situation.

You may have to concentrate to understand this story, because it is always difficult to talk about something so basic as this plan in clear, simple, and practical terms.

The original plan was to make life follow a simple process of going back and forth between two basic activities: creating chaos and restoring order. The two energetic and intelligent Siamese kitten leaders, Khaos and Kunfuzion, would create chaos and then order would be restored by the two wise and loving mice leaders, Klarity and Simplicity. Life would go back and forth between chaos and order. Chaos would involve confusing questions and complex possibilities to widen gaps while order would involve simple answers and clear certainties to close the gaps. This would never get boring, as there would always be a big enough supply of questions needing answers. This plan would bring constant and everlasting entertainment.

However, the kitten and mouse leaders were a bit worried that all the rest of the cats and mice would figure out such a simple plan too quickly and easily. That might make things too predictable and thus risk boredom. They needed some reinforcement to hide the plan. So the four leaders conspired to work together in an unlikely partnership.

On the one hand, the kitten leaders agreed to design some super powerful mental mousetraps to create much chaos, confusion, and complexity and keep all the mice very busy. That way they could maintain their illusion of being in control, take plenty of naps, and dream up more chaos.

On the other hand, the mouse leaders agreed to create simple solutions to help all the mice see clearer, think simpler, and sort through all this chaos. The mice needed this clarity and simplicity to avoid both the cats and the mousetraps. This would also keep all the mice busy looking for these solutions and trying to restore order to the chaos created by the cats. The important thing was that they could maintain their illusion of freedom. There would always be something to do for all the cats and the mice. As you can see, things were already starting to get confusing.

At this point something happened that most cats and mice would never know. The two kitten and two mouse leaders met secretly to implement the ultimate conspiracy: The other cats and mice would all be involved in creating chaos and restoring order, and they would never be sure which they were doing. The mousetraps would be big enough to catch cats and maybe even elephants and butterflies too! This was the master plan's climax. Even the four leaders themselves would be mixed up to make sure things remained interesting and fun for them too. They didn't realize it yet, but they had just redesigned life to keep everyone from being able to have their cheese and eat it too.

For the sake of simplicity and especially sanity, all the leaders decided first to allow cats to maintain the illusion of being in control by only thinking they were creating chaos, and then to allow mice to maintain their sense of freedom in restoring order without the unnecessary confusion of knowing they might be creating chaos too. This later reality would surely result in too much confusion for everyone, they all agreed. Besides, the story was already getting complicated enough without adding another layer of confusion.

By having everyone so involved in trying to create chaos and restore order and then not even being sure which task they were really carrying out, none of the cats or mice would be able to realize what he or she was actually doing. This way the basic plan would never be discovered. None of the cats or mice would be able to see the forest from the trees. The plan would be a safe, well-kept secret. Life would be fun, interesting, and meaningful in going back and forth between chaos and order, forever. There would be lots of challenges and rewards to keep things in perpetual motion. Cheese would be everywhere, but nowhere in particular.

Seven-Day Schedule

The ornery kitten leaders developed an ingenious seven-day schedule of designer mousetraps to kick off the plan. The idea was to declare *seven unwritten laws* which would assure the spreading of much chaos, confusion, and complexity and keep all the cats and mice so occupied they wouldn't know what they were doing.

Meanwhile, the mouse leaders were busy planting clear and simple answers and solutions to help restore order, which of course would just stimulate the need for more chaos. To make things interesting they hid clarity, simplicity, and order in unusual places, like in and near the mousetraps.

Of course, this plan was not all fully thought out before things got rolling. These things evolved naturally. They weren't fully developed beforehand because they were all just semiconscious thoughts of the kitten and mice leaders. That is typical in life—you are usually three-quarters the way to your destination before you know where it is you are going well enough to put a name to it. The other cats and mice learned this from the humans, whose educational institutions did the same thing.

Here is a preview of the mousetrap schedule:

Monday: Either-Orness. Monday's first unwritten law would dictate that everything be divided into opposites, being either this or that, right or wrong, good or bad, easy or difficult, comfortable or uncomfortable. On a large scale there would be life and death, and on a smaller scale there would be day and night. For right now, there would be here and there. There would be no balance between these opposite things; no one would be able to see the whole picture, so everyone would choose one side or the other and be convinced their side was best. There might even be some wanderlust for finding out what the other side was all about.

All mice and cats would either think or feel. They might be able to think about what they were doing, but since they weren't feeling it, it wouldn't make much sense being so abstract. If they felt the truth, it wouldn't make sense because it couldn't be translated into a thought. All chances of cats' and mice's happiness and success would be cut in half, and they could never be satisfied or feel complete. This nagging void would motivate both the cats and mice to create more chaos and try to restore order.

Tuesday: Unlikability. Beginning Tuesday, everyone would focus on everyone else's faults and complain about what everyone else needed to change rather than focus inwardly and make their own needed improvements. They would become selfish, impatient, controlling, quitting, and intolerant with others. Virtues like patience, kindness, humility, acceptance, and perseverance would be lost. Unlikability would result in bad relationships, and they, in turn, would result in unhealthy thinking and feeling. Of course, that would just spread more unlikability and increase poor relationships. This would occupy much time and effort that could be used to uncover the plan, keeping it safely hidden.

Wednesday: Babble. Midweek was always critical in both the cat and mouse worlds, so the four leaders put the mother-lode idea into this day. Many words and meanings would be developed Wednesday to keep all the cats and mice from communicating simply and clearly about what was going on. Miscommunication would make the chaos and confusion more chaotic and confusing, and the lack of listening would keep the clarity and simplicity that would uncover the plan from being communicated.

None of the cats or mice could communicate about what they thought or felt about what might be going on. They couldn't even communicate about all the miscommunication that was happening. Cats and mice would even misinterpret miscommunication and be convinced they were right and others were wrong. Basically, there wouldn't be any agreement about anything. Even the confusion would be confusing.

Thursday: Hide and Seek. On Thursday all the cats and mice would be afflicted with amnesia to forget what they were doing so they would keep on trying to create chaos and restore order without realizing it. None of the cats or mice would take responsibility for all the role-playing or games in which they were engaging to perpetuate the plan. None of them would even remember who they were or where they were going. Everybody would be playing a game to keep the plan going without even knowing it.

Friday: Duncery. Everyone's ability to think would be taken away Friday because of all the babble they had to use in order to think. Minds would keep re-babbling what their mouths started. Cats and mice would stop using creativity, intuition, and common sense and start assuming, being superficial, and staying close-minded. There would be no thinking about thinking, which might offer some clues about what was going on. Even if clear and accurate thoughts occurred, they couldn't be communicated clearly or accurately.

Saturday: Narcosis. On Saturday insensitivity would be sprinkled around to dull everyone's ability to tune into important insights and principles which might uncover the plan itself or what they were doing to keep it going. This would also keep everyone from getting proficient at either creating chaos or restoring order. The most important things would all be forgotten, and all the cats and mice would be paying attention to the unimportant things that would keep them from seeing what they needed to see, like how to get some decent sleep and how to avoid mousetraps. No one would know when the point of no return was coming and hence always go past it after it was too late to stop.

Sunday: Instantaneousmania. On Sunday, the world would start spinning faster and faster to make everything blurred. No cat or mouse would ever be able to see, hear, think, feel, or know what was going on. Cats and mice would be so dizzy from the speed they were moving they wouldn't think about their unthinking, understand their either-oring, communicate about their miscommunication, or even know the difference between chaos and order, not to mention not knowing which part they were playing.

All these mousetraps would work together to assure the secrecy of the plan and hide the awareness of what everyone was doing. For instance, all the cats and mice would be moving so quickly that they would never have the chance to think any quality thoughts or learn how to communicate better to discover what was going on. They would all be insensitive to important clues about what they might be doing, but they were not inclined to take responsibility for that, even if they might think it.

The smarter cats and mice who would eventually figure things out would be so sure they were right that their certainty and arrogance would cause a sufficient opposition on the other side to say they were wrong. Moreover, any clear and simple solutions that were discovered to reverse the mayhem created by these mousetraps would just serve to stimulate the further production of better mousetraps. The circle would never be broken.

These seven mousetraps all blend well together, like the single fibers on rope, to make one very big mousetrap to keep everyone from seeing the truth about what is going on. After all, if you aren't busy trying to get unstuck from the mousetrap you are already in, you are busy trying to avoid mousetraps altogether.

There isn't any time to think about important things, such as who you are and where you are going. Consequently, there will always be a gap between where you are and where you want to be.

If this all seems too confusing, slow down, become more sensitive, and think about the particular mousetrap in which you might now be stuck. Whether you are creating chaos, restoring order, or somewhere in between, these mental mousetraps are still part of what you are doing. If all this is clear and seems to be making too much sense, keep reading—you might find some amusing confusion.

MONDAY

1

Either-Orness

If you come to a fork in the road, take it.

—ex-Yankee mouse catcher

It was Monday morning, and the kittens had to get started. Being the smart one, Khaos had the initial flash of feline cerebral brilliance for the first day's response to the mouse problem. She didn't even have to ponder much because her thinking was greatly enhanced by the nutritional benefits of *Nine Lives*.

She addressed her stepbrother. "Well Kunfuzion," she began, "We must start by taking advantage of the limitations of mouse anatomy. Mice can only see 180 degrees at a time because, unlike us, they don't have eyes in the back of their heads. We will fool them into thinking they are always seeing everything all at once. That way they won't even know they are actually missing the other 180 degrees." She added, "They won't be able to see what is behind them unless they turn around, and then they still won't know what is behind them. What they know will be what they see, and what they see will only be half the picture."

Of course, they didn't even consider the issue of mice not being able to see in 3-D vision or beyond and all the other possibilities that visual enhancement posed. For right now, Khaos preferred to stick with a simple and clear version of confusion. Besides she didn't feel like getting involved in a deep discussion at this level of intellectual abstraction.

It took Kunfuzion, who was more street-wise and endowed with cat common sense, a little while to grasp the full implications of what his sister was saying. Eventually he remarked, "Yes, this is the most logical starting point to restore confusion to the mouse world and give us back our control. When a mouse is up, he won't know there is a down; and when some mice are wrong, they won't know what is right."

"Yes," said Khaos, adding, "when mice don't always see something important like cheese, they will begin to imagine it doesn't exist anymore. In effect, they will only be able to enjoy half of everything there is to achieve and enjoy. We will be cutting their success and happiness levels by 50 percent."

The cats then began to brainstorm all the specific things that would be categorized as either *this* or *that* to split things in half. The list grew too long, and knowing they were short on time, the cats decided they would just divide the entire mouse world in half with pairs of opposites to be named as the process evolved. To start out with there would be good and bad, right and wrong, normal and abnormal, rich and poor, thin and fat, and yang and yin.

Whichever side a mouse was on, he would be convinced that was the only place that existed. Since none of the mice could see the bigger 360-degree picture at one time, they would never know which side they were really on. When they might be wrong, they would be convinced they were right; and when they thought they were being good, they might really be being bad. They might even get confused about what side they saw other mice favoring. Since no mouse could see both sides of anything at once, there simply wouldn't be any certainty. "What magnificent confusion potential," both kittens proudly concluded. They had not realized it yet, but they had just invented dualistic thinking. The problem was that it would affect them too.

The two kittens had thought about things long enough and were ready to put the first day's plan into action. They bought a book of instructions on passing laws at their local cat mega-book store and worked together to draft their first new mouse law.

It was simple and to the point:

Law #1: Everything Has to Be Either This or That.

The kittens hired a professional lobbyist to help them present this first new law to the cat legislature. There wasn't any opposition, as all the cat population knew they had a serious mouse problem that needed a quick solution. They were all eager to see some confusion and control return, and they certainly did not want to be bothered by those bothersome mouse leaders Klarity and Simplicity. Deciding what was this and what was that would confuse plenty of little mice.

The new law was passed unanimously and put into effect instantly. Now the mouse world was divided in half. There was no wholeness or unity, only half-seeing, half-thinking, half-hearing and half-everything. "What a wonderfully deceiving illusion," thought Khaos and Kunfuzion, conveniently forgetting the impact this law was having on the cat world too. Mice won't be able to figure this one out. If they don't see mousetraps, they won't know they even exist. If they find some cheese one way, they won't know there are many other ways. They will automatically exclude half of all the possibilities, thinking they already have it all.

Within minutes confusion returned to the mouse world, and the cats were smiling again over their restored control. Mice argued over who was right and who was wrong. Some mice followed the rules while others broke them. Mice were convinced that if they didn't see something it didn't exist. Whatever a mouse thought, had to be true. Nothing could be true and false at the same time. Everything had to be either this or that. This was this, and that was that—or so it would appear to the either-oring mice. Everything was being divided in half and made much more complex than it needed to be.

Mayhem, muddle, and perplexity were well on their way to overtaking the mouse world on this gloomy Monday. Now, there were all sorts of strange and bizarre unbalanced behavior to play with too, as an unplanned, value-added side effect to this either-or thing. This was very entertaining for all the cats. Since there wasn't a middle to anything, mice could only see in one direction. They could go out as far on a limb as they dared and do whatever they wished because they weren't aware of where they were or what they were doing. They often forgot where their starting point was in anything they tried to do and subsequently forgot what they were trying to do and even where they were trying to go.

The affliction of this first deadly psychological sin was the start of all the major social problems of the mouse world. Mouse mental hospitals, drug treatment centers, eating disorder programs, and prisons quickly started bulging at the seams. The fallout from this first new mouse law was overwhelming, even for the most compassionate cats.

There were poor lost mice everywhere. There was no such thing as balance in anything. Everyone either worked too much or played too much. Unhealthy lifestyles and unfair practices were the norm in the mouse world. There was no such thing as assertiveness, only passive or aggressive behavior, which of course got mice nowhere but more frustrated.

Newspapers started carrying stories about mouse rage on the highways and drive-by mouse muggings. Of course, it was all over cheese. The weaker willy-nilly mice were passively giving their cheese away to the bullies. No mice knew how to ask for anything assertively. Mice had to be either passive or aggressive, right or wrong, or this or that. There wasn't any middle ground on which to compromise.

There were huge gaps between where mice were and where they wanted to be, but the mice couldn't see the gaps. Even if they could see them, they wouldn't have had a clue what to do to close the gaps. Either-oring mice could never see what they needed to see because all the important stuff was always within the other 180 degrees they weren't seeing. Confusion and complexity were everywhere; Klarity and Simplicity were seen nowhere. Now Khaos and Kunfuzion felt a little more in control. They decided they could take long catnaps. They both stretched and yawned.

By Monday afternoon though, there were two different developments happening in opposite areas of the mouse world. While Khaos and Kunfuzion were busy spreading either-orness around, the two mice leaders, Klarity and

Simplicity, were doing their job by planting anti-either-orness solutions here and there.

On the East Coast there were two different groups of rebel mice who started questioning things. One group wanted the mice to start thinking with both sides of their brains, and the other group wanted all mice to work toward self-development. The first group was getting tired of logic, rationality, and convergent thinking. All this left-brain activity was making them feel lopsided. They were always taking left turns and no right ones. This got boring. Mice wanted to know what was to the right.

The second group was growing tired of being stressed out from too much work and becoming unhealthy from too much eating, drinking, smoking, lack of exercise, and other self-abuse. This group began imagining the mice could be in much better condition. After all, even mice had growth potential. A fully self-actualized mice world was this group's goal. They believed it was do-able.

On the West Coast, the hard work of a few smart mouse statisticians started to pay off. They began crunching numbers from their general observations and making inferences from their data manipulations. Somehow they were making some sense out of all this nonsense. They quickly revealed indisputable proof that there were actually 360 degrees to the big picture. Their charts and graphs dazzled even the most cynical and myopic mice.

The realization that mice were missing one half of everything was a mind-boggling revelation that would have far-reaching effects on the mouse world. Mice were getting excited about the possibilities of doubling their success and happiness by adding another 180 degrees to their field of vision. Talk about mind-expanding! They questioned why they had thought they knew it all before when, in fact, they had only been seeing half the picture. This was a humbling experience to say the least.

Khaos and Kunfuzion got word of these disturbing events through their mouse intelligence program by early evening. Realizing the next stage would be for the mice to begin to get a glimpse of the other half of things and recognize Klarity and Simplicity through the confusion fog that had been temporarily restored, they knew another part of the master plan needed to be implemented.

However, they also knew they had a little wiggle time because it would take the mice at least a few hours to finish the time-consuming job of putting all the halves of everything back together again. So Khaos and Kunfuzion could get a night's rest before they had to start thinking of a new way to keep the mice from finding their unconfused influential mouse leaders. "Phew," meowed Khaos. The nearby Kunfuzion just yawned.

TUESDAY

2

Unlikability

Be what you is, not what you ain't, 'cause if you ain't what you is, you is what you ain't.

—famous mouse musician

Tuesday morning came around faster than Khaos would have liked; nevertheless, she and her brother both knew they had some serious thinking to do. This time they held a meeting to come up with Tuesday's plan to restore all the confusion that Klarity and Simplicity had helped the mice sort through during the night.

The mice had rejoined many of the opposites they didn't even know were part of the same thing. They began to see right in wrong and wrong in right and how such things as creativity and logic could work together in a complementary fashion. Several new words were developed to reflect a bigger picture—words such as *coopetition*, *effecticiency*, and *creatuitivity*. Mice even started to think as one unified mouse race. A few exceptionally smart mice had peak experiences at seeing in 3-D. These unconfusing occurrences were not good for the cat world. The meeting was now open for discussion, and coffee was being served, with whipped cream and catnip, naturally.

This time it was Kunfuzion who spoke first. "I have an idea," he said confidently. "Let's divert the mice's attention from their thinking to their actions.

"What does that mean?" asked Khaos. She was beginning to wonder what her brother had been eating. She had also noticed the litter box wasn't the same lately.

Kunfuzion quickly answered, "We will make mice act unlikable by passing a law against being likable."

Khaos thought about the idea for a minute or two and began to see all sorts of possibilities. "You mean things like having a negative attitude, being aloof, and acting unfriendly?" she asked.

"Yes, and other things like over-reacting, being moody, showing low energy, being unkind, and speeding around not paying any attention to anyone else for any length of time."

"Okay," said Khaos, "But we will need to keep mice from focusing on themselves or they will eventually be able to see their own unlikability. We have to make sure they only focus on everybody else's unlikability."

Kunfuzion agreed but proactively added, "We also better have a back-up plan for when mice do focus on themselves, as that is bound to happen eventually. When they do, they'll be convinced that they are something very special and unique from all other mice. They will also be even more convinced that their 180-degree perspectives are much better than any other mouse's. We'll call it *egomania*. We can even make some money off their need to have vanity plates on their little mouse mobiles and mirrors in their mouse holes. Now let's go circulate a petition to get some support for this second mouse law. I think we have something here."

Both kittens liked shifting mice's attention from their thinking to the more powerful feelings that would be associated with things they disliked about others. They predicted Klarity and Simplicity would be of no help at all on this particular affliction. Both purred loudly.

They went off and got a couple of million cat paw signatures, and before anybody knew it, the second new mouse law was in effect:

Law #2: Likability Is Outlawed.

Soon the second deadly psychological affliction was passed around. Negativity, unfriendliness, unhelpfulness, selfishness, and other unlikable things became common. Unlikable personality traits like immaturity, bragging, and cynicism replaced virtues such as gentleness, patience, and perseverance. Obnoxious and repulsive personalities surfaced everywhere, including chronic whiners and complainers, know-it-all show-offs, up-tight perfectionists, narrow-minded prudes, drama-stirring queens, promise-breakers, and backstabbers, just to mention a few—and these unlikable types could be found in the best mouse houses.

Mice didn't understand how being likeable could make other things easier, but then again, they could only see all the other mice's unlikability. There was no self-focusing (except for obnoxious egomania) to help them see their own unlikable behavior, such as not sharing cheese or not taking the time to ask other mice how they were doing. Simple niceness was fading.

Relationships at home and at work were complete disasters. Nobody wanted to make needed changes to improve likability. Mice spent all their time trying to change other mice's unlikability. This involved complaining about all the inappropriate behavior of criticizing, belittling, and even yelling. Mice were trying all sorts of different ways to control each other. This wasn't good because even mice valued their freedom.

All trust began to dissolve. The only choices still left from the first affliction were to control or be controlled. There were never any positive results from all these inappropriate exchanges, and mice ended up with nothing but anger and frustration. Unlikability spread considerable more confusion on top of the confusion already left over from all the eitherorness divisions that were not put back together earlier.

However, this diversion was not quite enough to keep hiding Klarity and Simplicity, forever. Mice grew weary of feeling all the time and not getting to think. When a mouse got uncomfortable enough about something, he or she did something to change the situation for the better. Sometimes it took more discomfort than usual, but this wasn't the case with this unlikability thing. Unlikability wasn't a normal state, even for mice.

Actually in fairness to Khaos and Kunfuzion, it was only the beginning of the week, and so these young mischievous Siamese kittens weren't at full speed yet. They didn't put much effort into planning or implementing this unlikability law, and the results of this lack of effort showed quickly. They kind of slacked-off, being overly confident in the dramatic and far-reaching effects of Monday's eithor-orness affliction. They realized from hindsight that they may have put all their marbles in one bag. In a sense, they fell prey to their own brand of either-orness: The unlikability mousetrap would either work well or it wouldn't.

In reality most mice just practiced mild forms of unlikabilty, and so this second new mouse law didn't have the full impact for which the cats had hoped. In retrospect that was ironic, because unlikability was mainly an attitude, and attitudes were what drove behavior. If you want to produce confused behavior, start with confusing attitudes, Khaos had originally thought.

The idea probably would have worked better if Khaos and Kunfuzion had put more effort into planning and implementing it. Taking the time to ask for input from the mice would have helped too, especially from Klarity and Simplicity. The kittens hadn't anticipated the mice's mediocre reaction to unlikability either. This was a middle position to which they didn't think the mice were capable of getting. They were wrong. Oh well, on to the next part of the plan. "We can still fix this," Khaos assured her brother.

WEDNESDAY

3

Babble

I know you believe you understand what you think I said, but I am not sure you realize that what you heard is not what I meant.

—mouse graffiti

Despite the cat leaders' first two attempts to hide Klarity and Simplicity with either-orness and unlikability mousetraps, these two pesky mice kept showing up in enough places that the other mice were beginning to talk again. Mouse hope started growing, and that was always a warning sign for the cats. Klarity and Simplicity seemed to be getting quite resistant and resilient for some reason. Perhaps it was something in their cheese.

This imminent situation worried Khaos and Kunfuzion because they had both already invested much time and effort on this important project. After all, the more you put into something, the more you expect in return. (This truth later started a mouse gambling business out West.) Unfortunately the kitten's first two confusion interventions were beginning to lose their controlling effect. It was mid-week and time to conjure up some serious confusion. They felt a need to do something drastic.

After considerable thought, Khaos decided to go away to read some books and get a few advanced degrees in nebulous uncertainty, entangled complexity, tentative ambiguity, and other eruditely confusing things like that. It was time to pull out all the stops. She withdrew some cash from her money market account to pay for tuition. It would be a wise investment.

In a few hours she came back, fully armed with an impressive advanced degree in Ultimate Perplexity and said, "Well, Kunfuzion, I have a grand idea. This new deadly psychological sin of mine will put both Klarity and Simplicity down for the count! I have the Mercedes of all mousetraps!" Khaos was proud of herself.

"How does it work?" asked a slightly puzzled Kunfuzion.

Khaos could hardly contain herself, "We shall pass the third law that makes babble the only permissible language, and while we're at it, we will make listening a crime." She was so pleased with herself that her eyes criss-crossed twice.

"Gee, Khaos, all those books and education make you the top confusion consultant in the world! This is a great plan. You are a genius," concluded Kunfuzion.

"I know," boasted Khaos. "Let's go to the cat legislature and get this new law enacted."

Off the two kittens scampered, confident that they had finally figured a way to never have to hear about Klarity and Simplicity anymore. Mice would again be confused, and the cats would be back in control. Talk about deserving a catnap!

By now Khaos and her brother had made good progress at perfecting the process of getting new laws passed without opposition. They started a new law-passing division in their Kumpany, and so it didn't take long to get the new babble law passed.

Law #3: Babble Is the Only Permissible Language, and Listening Is a Crime.

There was no dissent because all the other cats had total faith in their confusion heroes, Khaos and Kunfuzion. Besides all the cats were still a little confused themselves from the first two anti-Klarity and no Simplicity laws. Hence, this third new mouse law was easily passed. All mice now had to speak in confusing babble, and no mouse was permitted to listen.

In a weak moment, a special interest group added an amendment to the law, allowing mice to listen but only to respond. No understanding allowed. That actually turned out to be a good technique. It tricked mice and added more confusion. It worked well. Miscommunication was everywhere. Miscommunication was even misunderstood, and that doubled the confusion because misunderstanding could only be mis-communicated more. There was no chance of any understanding. None at all.

For hours, Klarity and Simplicity were totally invisible and inaudible. Mice became masters at talking and writing reams of manuscripts and memos and saying nothing. There were tons of books, training programs, videos, audiotapes, and workbooks full of complex, chaotic, complicated "ideation" that meant absolutely nothing at all.

Mice also created an abundance of effective distractions to keep from hearing one another. They started paying more attention to their own internal pre-occupations about confusion and distorting all incoming information by the perceptual biases of their own individual preferences for confusion. They became impatient for getting more confusion. Verbal confusion was the main currency for all mouse transactions.

Some mice formed special groups. One became especially skilled at creating defensive climates that totally shut down communication. Their techniques were being accusing, judgmental, superior, and controlling. They replaced the word "I" with "You." This helped replace the growing practice of assertiveness with unbalanced aggression and passivity once again, which in turn increased unlikability. Not being able to communicate about unlikability just made it worse.

Another group went around changing definitions of words in dictionaries without telling anyone else. For that matter, no one was allowed to communicate clearly, so these mischievous acts weren't ever discovered. This devious group also invented word connotations just in case the new dictionary definitions of certain words didn't adequately confuse mice. Words could now have unspoken and hidden meanings.

There were "good" words and "bad" words, and there were "strong and fast" sentences and "weak and slow" paragraphs. These word opposites managed to bring back some either-or thinking again. Naturally, there was no consistency in any usage or interpretations. A very tall "Tower of Babble" was designed by mouse engineers and constructed with part-time mouse labor.

These sneaky little acts were very clever, because now simple principles like truth, honesty, goodness, success, normality, and happiness couldn't be understood, even if they were somehow discovered. They meant something different to each mouse who wrote, spoke, heard, or read the words. This separate word reality was the beginning of something big. There was reality, and then there was the reality that words created. Khaos and Kunfuzion were watching, wide-eyed at all the great consequences of their babble mousetrap. It was more than they had hoped for.

Regarding these emerging separate realities, they called the first one *real reality* and the second *artificial reality*. There even had to be a reality to determine which of these was correct, but the trouble was to know the side from which the word descriptions themselves were coming. And thanks to the earlier introduction of dualistic thinking, that reality itself had to be either correct or incorrect ad infinitum. Fortunately, the mice were unable to go any further than that. Actually, few made it that far.

Then, of course, there were the mass communication groups. They convinced everyone that "more is better," and that notion really added to the confusion. There was more information than could ever be consumed in mouse libraries reserved for confusing information. Then an especially bright mouse group kept finding ways to get their nanosecond machines to produce information faster than mice could keep up with it. What a mess!

The resulting insurmountable mountain of mayhem required a huge amount of space and time. In fact, there wasn't much space or time left at all. The mice would have complained, but they weren't able to communicate about any of this in a quality manner or ask questions that would have challenged the information maker's viewpoint. They couldn't talk about what needed to be talked about most.

A particularly subversive and devious mouse group invented what they called *non-verbal communication*. Mice started making all sorts of wild assumptions about what a mouse was or wasn't saying by over-interpreting clues such as hand and face gestures, tone of voice, use of silence, body positioning, fidgeting, etc. The other mice started believing they could actually understand what all this non-verbal communication was, verbally. This practice alone was a major contributor to the skyrocketing mouse divorce rate. Now it didn't matter what a mouse was saying or meaning to say—it was just *how* he or she was saying it.

A small group of creative mouse writers developed new figurative speech. This was a special version of confusing non-verbal communication with layered meanings. They introduced many colorful and interesting new ways of saying things, such as similes, oxymorons, panaches, neologisms, personifications, and puns. Phrases such as "smooth as glue," "eloquent silence," "Hoppy Thanksgobble Day," "rightsizing," "the eye of a hurricane," and "I right wrong" were strategically placed in written documents and speeches.

Mouse thinking was getting blurred more and more by all this word confusion, and mice couldn't listen to anything that might be less confusing. They just wasted time trying to communicate important, helpful ideas because no one else was listening to understand. They vaguely wondered why they weren't getting anywhere. All the mice just kept going round and round in a vicious circle. Mental illness was becoming so prevalent again in the mouse world, that all the government institutions started releasing them all back to the community, thinking that was a workable solution. "Next they would release mouse criminals to half-way houses right in our neighborhoods," silently thought a few critical mice.

One thing that closed the door was the subtle but powerful injunction against communicating about communication. Confusion was very contagious and inter-related. Mice could be confused and confused about being confused. They could even be confused about being confused about being confused. But there was no communicating about that confusion to get unconfused. That was the point where most mice passed out. The on-line chat rooms and bulletin boards also had their share of casualties. Actually it was a lion's share, since there were no rules in cyberspace.

The amazing thing about this third law was that it affected everything the mice were doing. Mice couldn't communicate their confusion and couldn't even think about it, let alone do something about it. They couldn't even listen for feint whispers of Klarity or Simplicity. This law put a lock on the problem once and for all. There was no way out of this one. Khaos and Kunfuzion had finally succeeded in hiding Klarity and Simplicity forever. It was time for a major nap.

THURSDAY

4

Hide and Seek

If all the world is a stage, I want to operate the trap door.
—retired mouse movie director

While the cats were sleeping, the mice did play. Mouse thinkers began to attack babble with their writing. Again, all the mice were beginning to get uncomfortable enough about this babble mousetrap to be motivated to do something about it, just as they did with the unlikability trap.

Additionally, they were inspired by earlier mouse artists from the painting and music fields who ingeniously figured out how to communicate important truths and useful ideas by using unusual images, colorful metaphors, and other creative techniques to suggest deeper meaning. They knew mice wouldn't understand anything important if they just looked for literal meaning. Mice had to be encouraged to go a little deeper below the surface. After all, something could mean one thing to all the mice, and then really mean something else to each one of them individually. Words were words, but they had meanings.

Then the mouse newspaper/magazine companies and book publishers learned the fine art of word bites. They started experimenting with high-impact headlines and mesmerizing book covers that really attracted mice as they walked by. Both these media industries became quite successful at clarifying complex confusion with simple, clear phrases that caught mice's immediate attention. Covers sold books, and headlines sold newspapers.

Of course, the advertising agencies quickly followed with their clever, money-making slogans and jingles. This was communication at its finest. Powerful ideas were being expertly packaged to make sure listeners and viewers were "being all they could be" and "knowing where they wanted to go tomorrow." Words had to be carefully chosen to guarantee mega-impact and avoid any chance of misunderstanding or ambiguity. The quicker you could say it, the better. Words that carried vivid images were especially effective.

Some skilled resume writers started teaching job candidates how to summarize their 25-year careers clearly and succinctly on a single page. Communication experts were coaching mouse politicians how to become more believable and likable. Many simple and clear ideas were beginning to get communicated by writers helping mouse couples develop better interpersonal skills. These developments were capped off by the fantastic video-music clips and big-screen movie previews. This technologically-enhanced communication was totally awesome and inspired better communication by even average mice.

The tower of babble was beginning to lean precariously. Khaos and Kunfuzion, both realized their backs were against the wall once again, despite the first three days of hard work. Kunfuzion was away on a much-needed vacation in the Bahamas, so the two had to schedule a long-distance phone call to discuss what to do to regain their confusion momentum over the mice. Fortunately, Khaos had a 90-minute Cat-Mart calling card.

They brainstormed on the phone for an hour and came up with a clever new mousetrap design for restoring confusion. They would teach the mice how to play the game of hide and seek and not bother telling them it was just a game. They would encourage some mice to hide so well they could never be found, while convincing others to always hide where they could be easily found.

This hide-and-seek game turned out to be a subtle way of reinforcing the earlier either-or affliction and dividing the mice world into more opposing groups. Now there could be optimists and pessimists, adventurers and non-adventurers, and liberals and conservatives. There would even be teams of hiders and teams of seekers to hide unlikable mice and find likable ones.

Khaos and Kunfuzion ended the phone conversation on an exceptionally upbeat note. Kunfuzion then returned to the beach and his mouse-ritas, while Khaos put the machinery in motion to get the fourth new mouse law passed and enacted. Within minutes, the fourth new mouse law was posted:

Law #4: Everyone Can Play Hide and Seek but Can't Know It Is Just a Game.

This was where Khaos was at her best. Her cat imagination ran wild with an unending supply of hide-and-seek games. First she and Kunfuzion would have mice do the amnesia game in which they would completely forget basic things like who they where, what they were doing, where they were going, and why. Mice would not remember their own basic identity. They wouldn't remember what they had forgotten, especially where they could go when they needed help. "How more confusing can you get than that?" mused Kunfuzion.

Then, of course, there was the special edge game that Khaos authored while on an earlier cruise but never had the opportunity to use. This was the subtle little game that mice would play by tiptoeing up to the very edge just to see how far they could get without falling off. The socially acceptable mice would play edge games such as skydiving, white-water rafting, and mountain climbing, and make careers as politicians, entertainers, professional athletes, and dotcom entrepreneurs. Average mice prepared resumes at work, cheated on their income taxes, told little white lies to their friends, engaged in mild road rage, and committed occasional acts of adultery.

The socially unacceptable mice played treacherous edge games with drugs, severe forms of mental illness, poverty, crime, homelessness, prostitution, and over- and under-eating. The edge-game players didn't know it, but playing the edge game was like risking drowning by holding your breath under water. There was a twilight period when you could totally lose consciousness without ever knowing it.

The mice quickly developed other fun edge games themselves. These were games like making up excuses as to why they didn't have enough cheese, rationalizing their poor performance in not knowing where new cheese might be, role-playing in hiding cheese and finding mouse traps, and the most fun edge game of all—reality zone surfing.

By now the babble affliction had produced a variety of reality zones for mice. They could visit the physical zone where they knew things that touched their physical senses like seeing, hearing, smelling, and touching; and they could visit the psychological zone where they could think about things and make mouse mental interpretations. This was the invention of psychobabble.

Mice could also visit the artificial reality zone that was imposed and controlled by their own words and "big brother," and also the spiritual zone where the cats enjoyed watching mice interact with each other from different reality zones. This was miscommunication at its best.

Confusion was impossible to avoid, and uproar was the usual result. Nobody realized the effect of the zone from which the communication was coming.

There were side benefits to all these hide-and-seek games. Mice easily got into overplaying roles such as parent-child, teacher-student, boss-subordinate, Catholic-Protestant, and Democrat-Republican. They could even carry the roles they learned well to other playing fields. In the mouse stage of life, all the mice were becoming Academy Award nominees. Role-playing script writing even became a new mouse industry.

For the mice who hid too well, there was anxiety and separation fear of not being found, and the ones who were always found right away worried, complained, had low self-esteem, and were co-dependent. Since mice had also hidden their own responsibility from themselves, they couldn't do anything constructive, which would have alleviated the worrying, complaining, fear and anxiety. Mouse paranoia and panic neuroticism added more forms of mental illness to the mouse world, and the mouse pharmaceutical stock prices rose astronomically.

The confusing thing about these hide-and-seek games were the gnawing feelings mice were having that suggested they could eventually do something if they really wanted to. The trouble was, they had forgotten who was in charge of their own destiny. They were also getting out of practice accepting any ownership for playing all these entertaining games. That carried too much responsibility for the mice who were already too busy being confused.

By early evening, Kunfuzion added a last-minute contribution with his *wussiness* peripheral hide-and-seek mousetrap device. This upgrade allowed mice to get weak and quit things easily without being overly concerned about the consequences. Quitting became so popular that mice were unable to quit quitting. This had a major impact on cheese prices and the mouse stock market. Oddly they called it the "bull" market.

The mice occupied themselves completely with all these fun hide-and-seek games, getting more confused through the night as the cats slept peacefully. Many mice got totally lost in the roles they were loudly over-playing, and others fell off the edge completely. The ruckus or thumps didn't wake up the cats though.

FRIDAY

5

Duncery

If you can't change your mind,
are you sure you even have one?
—mouse bumper sticker

Things remained fairly confusing for a few hours, especially with all the mice scurrying around playing a variety of hide-and-seek games and then denying any knowledge of playing those games. But unfortunately for the cats, something significant was developing at a nearby mouse community of college teachers on Friday morning.

One of Klarity's many offspring, Basix, invented a new and unusual form of positive thinking. This new variety wasn't at all like the older version where a mouse would simply replace a negative thought with a positive one. Basix explained, "That would be like when you used to say, 'I'm not really hungry for this delicious piece of raspberry double chocolate cheesecake,' when your sweet tooth was really craving it."

The professor continued, "With this new type of positive thinking you would say, 'I am going to have a small piece of this irresistibly scrumptious cheese cake—and then go exercise at the mouse gym with my friend in the morning.'" The new positive thinking was win-win for everyone, without dreadful either-or, win-lose choices. This was the best assault on dualistic thinking ever made in the mouse world. This might even expose hiders-and-seekers and either-orers.

With the encouragement of more new positive thinking, a young psychologically-trained mouse turned an intriguing older engineering term, *perturbation point*, into an entire self-management system. Originally these "P" points were the few critical stress points in a structure, which facilitated implosion for easier demolition.

He later expanded this notion into *psychological power points.* These were hidden miniature versions of the original creative process of the Universe. "P" points stimulated virtually unlimited creative problem-solving solutions. They could be useful insights, valuable wisdom, practical principles, or just routine activities. This was quite a fantastic discovery—and all by serendipity! *Serendipity* was one of Khaos' favorite words, which just meant accidentally finding something more valuable than what you were actually looking for.

The mouse shrink showed many mice how they could apply these magical "P" points into a simple art of being smart. "P" points," this smart mouse lectured during the Mouse Annual Psychological Association Convention, "are small but intense, well-timed and well-placed interventions that produce major results. They are simple but powerful clues for making progress at anything. They are the little keys you can use to open big doors."

He summarized, "Some common examples are newspaper headlines, book covers, advertising jingles, and political sound bites. A big personal "P" point is the attitude you have in reaction to getting your cheese moved." "Hmms" spread noisily through the large audience. Excitement was brewing.

"P" point management took off as the self-development program of choice for the new mouse millennium. Mice weren't just rethinking old thoughts differently, they were actually beginning to have entirely new and unique thoughts. "P"-point sensitivity was on the increase, and that in turn stimulated even more creative thinking and even the reuse of intuition, which had disappeared over the last few days. What was happening was termed "breakthrough thinking."

An important and useful spin to this new positive thinking soon surfaced. It had to do with a mouse's mental conflict between *inclusion* and *exclusion*. In the past, mice typically excluded new information that did not agree or fit with what they already knew or believed. This was their self-imposed tunnel vision island that missed all the water around it. The opposite practice, inclusion, quickly became a popular add-on to the new positive-thinking fad. Inclusion wasn't "either-or" dividing; it was "and-and" adding.

Now mice would look for ways to figure out how they could include another mouse's information or point of view into their own knowledge and then open up bigger and wider doors to learn more and more. And all they had to do was go back to a point of common consensus and work together from there to add agreeable bits of information. They could concentrate their positive energy in finding agreement while losing their negative energy previously used to find disagreement. The net gain was a big boost in mouse energy.

Why hadn't they thought of this before they invented hundreds of different mouse religions and so many other things that divided the world in small opposing parts? That was just the tip of the iceberg. They thought about all the needless multiple choices they had unthinkingly invented for a single thing. What unnecessary confusion they had unknowingly propagated on themselves. Why did they think they needed over a hundred different styles of mouse running shoes? They didn't know it yet, but *quality* was about to replace *quantity* in the mouse world's vocabulary.

This inclusion thing started making all the mice feel like one team working toward a common goal that would benefit them all. Vague memories of the earlier either-or mousetrap strengthened their conviction. "No more separation fear or alienation anxiety for mice," thought Klarity and Simplicity still in hiding. Other mice were exploring how to include positive aspects of egomania and hide-and-seek amnesia, and the mice management gurus were starting to see many excellent inclusion training opportunities with this "P" Point concept. Basix was eventually nominated for a Mice Nobel Peace Prize for her valuable cognitive contribution. Klarity was very proud. His little mouse heart was doing flip-flops.

This present state of affairs alarmed both Khaos and Kunfuzion. If mice were to figure out how to manage their personal "P" points to close gaps, to think positively, and to include more valuable information from other mice, they would soon figure out how to get back in touch with Klarity and Simplicity. This would be disastrous. The wall of confusion and misunderstanding the cats had worked so hard to build and maintain would come tumbling down with just a few puffs.

"We must think really hard to come up with an infallible way to keep mice from seeing or hearing or thinking about Klarity and Simplicity!" exclaimed Khaos in a frenzied state. "We need a Rolls Royce of mousetraps that will produce micro-minded, brain draining, mental impotence," she chanted. She was more nervous than she had ever been before. Even Kunfuzion noticed her agitation. "Perhaps too much table food for the finicky eater," thought her brother to himself.

In a rather unusual instance of academic intelligence, Kunfuzion nodded and posed an interesting thought, "What if we don't allow mice to think very well?"

"Hmm," replied Khaos, "That has some potential for being a deadly psychological sin. We shall ban all critical thinking. That way Klarity and Simplicity will never even be thought about."

Kunfuzion humbly reminded Khaos, "I don't think you can end a sentence with a preposition."

But Khaos, not being inclined to allow herself to become overly burdened with details of grammar or spelling, despite her high IQ, retorted, "Oh well, we can't think about insignificant things like that anymore." She sensed she might even be on to something bigger and better regarding the interaction between miscommunication and unthinking in general, but the two had much work to do with this new no critical thinking law. It was Friday, and this was the last workday before the weekend.

Khaos and Kunfuzion spent the next few hours crafting all the details of the un-thinking law. Khaos rambled on about such things as mandatory assuming and brain surgery of the perceptual processes to make mice believe in the artificial certainties and premature closures they were over-simplifying. Kunfuzion just scratched his head. Khaos also spoke of orchestrating many unsolvable paradoxes and introducing the concept of paradigm-morphing. Kunfuzion scratched his head again.

With her usual flair for anticipating objections to her abstract intellectual concepts and 15-letter words, Khaos knew she had some explaining to do, especially regarding clarification of these first two brain-related mouthfuls. She decided to provide a real-life example of how the brain could oversimplify things by just filling in the gaps with anything and still have the illusion of certainty. Kunfuzion was getting intrigued even though he didn't quite understand where this was going.

Khaos challenged the other cats with a scheme to make a million dollars in one day. This certainly got their typical cat curiosity level up in the red zone. She instructed, "Put a contest notice in the local mouse newspaper, charging mice $10 for submitting a solution to the following riddle and offering them $100 for the correct answer. They can even pass it on to their friends via e-mail. Here it is:

> *This riddle must be done in your head without paper or pencils. Take 1,000 and add 40 to it. Now add another 1,000. Now add 30 and then another 1,000. Now add 20, now add another 1,000. Now add 10. What is the answer?*

For the benefit of the cats, Khaos whispered, "It is *not* 5,000!" (That was the brain's normal simplified result.) Kunfuzion kept his answer to himself, which turned out to be a smart move. Lots of other cats were about to get rich, though. It could even be the start of a new multi-level marketing scheme over the Internet. "Unlimited possibilities," ruminated the entrepreneurial cats. Dollar signs registered in their cat eyes.

Regarding the last two complicated unthinking ideas Khaos had previously mentioned, Kunfuzion had a vague idea regarding this paradox thing from earlier discussions but was a little unclear about the paradigm-morphing concept. He had to ask the dumb question, "What's that?"

Khaos was a patient teacher and spotted a teaching moment. She skillfully directed Kunfuzion to identify a few key viewpoints he was sure of and then challenged him with a pointed question, "If you move locations from where you are looking at something, won't that change the appearance of what you are seeing?" (She wondered why her brother had forgotten all the similar ramifications from the earlier 180-degree, either-or law. Maybe her brother was becoming chronologically challenged, she thought to herself, hoping he couldn't read her mind.)

Kunfuzion still wasn't quite clear about all this abstract thinking. Khaos knew that she needed to come up with a more concrete example to help him make the connection. She continued, "Do you remember when mice thought the world was flat, and they worried that if they went too far they would fall off the edge?" "Oh yes," replied Kunfuzion, having a light-bulb moment, "Some mouse country funded a voyage to see how far they could get. They ended up sailing way past the imagined edge and finally realized there wasn't any edge of the world at all. They discovered the world was actually round without any edges. I think that opened up the cheese trade."

"Yes," said Khaos, "It is like trying to measure something with a rubber ruler, you get a whole new perspective each time." This went right over Kunfuzion's head, but enough of the other explanation stuck. Kunfuzion thought about a clever saying he had once heard—something like trying to roll a ball of molasses up a sand hill, but he couldn't figure out how to work that in. At any rate, the two Siamese kittens were now ready to get the ball rolling on the new law.

By now, Khaos and Kunfuzion were becoming skilled lobbyists themselves, and so they were easily able to get the fifth new mouse law passed and enacted within minutes.

Law #5: No More Quality Thinking, Only Duncery.

This new law was so good, it even made the headlines of the *NY Times*. Of course, it was given a few nights on *Mouse King Live*, too.

Soon after this law was passed, bewilderment, bafflement and perplexity spread like a wild fire. Mental laziness was a big hit with the mice. Mice were once again convincing themselves that something had to be either clear or unclear, right or wrong, good or bad; but whatever side they joined, they couldn't deny the possibility of the other side being right. If we are right, then you *have* to be wrong. If you are right, then we *have* to be wrong. We can't possibly both be right and wrong or neither. They had forgotten the earlier art of positive thinking and inclusion, not to mention "P" points.

Mice stopped asking any questions because that would challenge whatever wrong beliefs they had which they were convinced were correct. Their temporary fix to this problem was to only ask a few questions to which they already had the answers. They started making all kinds of wild assumptions without feeling the slightest need to verify any of their new information. Their brains developed a lazy way of answering questions their mouths should have been asking. For instance, if some particular brand of cheese wasn't in their favorite cheese store, they just assumed it wasn't being produced anymore.

Mice, not being able to think about their own thinking, were unable to notice that they had lost common sense and were making many thinking mistakes, such as over-generalizing, oversimplifying, and even fatal thinking. This later thinking error caused a large group of mice to be diagnosed with a new form of mental illness. This was confusingly summarized in The *Mouse DSM IX* for educated mice. Common symptoms were thoughts such as, "If I can't do this, there must be something wrong with me," and "Nobody else has thoughts like these, so I must be abnormal." Their only response was to try to be normal in abnormal ways, which only made them appear more abnormal.

With all these other laws, being normal was impossible. And not being able to think or communicate clearly, mice got stuck chasing their tails inside vicious circles. There was no more new positive thinking, "P" points, or inclusion; back to negativity, insensitivity to "P" points, and exclusion. Without critical thinking, mice were unable to solve problems or resolve conflicts. All they could do was scratch their heads in mouse wonderment. Soon there were more problems and conflicts than there were mice. Both convergent and divergent thinking ended up at the same place: Nowhere.

Eventually this unthinking epidemic rejuvenated an older business. Somebody had to take care of the poor, pitiful, mentally-ill mice. Most mice became convinced that if thinking caused problems, then thinking must cease. This conclusion seemed fairly reasonable. Both Khaos and Kunfuzion fell over laughing at that one. On the other hand, mouse drug reps saw another opportunity, and it wasn't an hour before over-the-counter anti-thinking drugs were available.

Mouse self-help books flooded the mouse bookstores. A mouse version of the earlier human *Escalen Institute* reopened on the West Coast. But these pitiful responses only helped to spread more confusion. There was nothing worse than an un-thinking mouse group leader, reformed mouse therapist, or egotistical author who thought he had figured out everything, and now all the other mice needed his solutions. After all, people like this only wrote self-help books to sort out their own confusion. And teachers only taught because they could not do anything else.

Then an unexpected side effect to this new law kicked in. Even Khaos hadn't anticipated the benefit of this development. Mice started getting their thoughts and feelings mixed up. What they were thinking, they were really feeling; and what they were feeling, they were really thinking. This created another unsolvable paradox. And then, of course, there were groups of mice feelers and groups of mice thinkers who were convinced they were right. Thoughts and feelings got totally tangled up, and there were major battles trying to untangle them. These battles kept going for hours.

Khaos and Kunfuzion thought their work was done with this fifth deadly psychological sin, and now they could enjoy the weekend. "Mice will never be able to think their way out of this confusion and complexity," they both beamed. They were becoming the elite confusion experts of the cat world. They even appeared on the cat world's version of Oprah and Leno to discuss their new book. Off to another long nap. It was well deserved. But unfortunately it was a bit premature. When the cats slept, the mice started playing again. By the wee hours of the morning, many mice were beginning to have a few quality thoughts again. There were even some "ah-ha" moments.

SATURDAY

6

Narcosis

You can see a lot by observing.
—same ex-Yankee mouse catcher

The two kittens had to begin their weekend on the wrong foot. They had to work. Being proactive, they didn't want to risk any significant improvement in over-all mouse thinking. The cats preferred that the majority of mice stay 12 short of a baker's dozen in brainpower. They had to have another meeting to add some more oomph to their chaos conspiracy.

Kumplexity, one of the new staff members the two kitten leaders had recruited, spoke first. He said, "I have an idea." "Let's hear it," replied Khaos and Kunfuzion in unison. That was after they yawned, slightly. "What if we were to hide all the simple and clear principles that would help mice to find Klarity and Simplicity and then make another law banning mice from discovering any of these principles. We can hide the most valuable principles inside tricky paradoxes and right under the mice's noses. I read an article in the *Cat Digest* that said it takes awhile to notice the obscure, but the obvious, even longer." The Far Eastern cats called these riddles *Koans*. They went around asking simple but wise questions like, "Who are you?" This would surely be too direct and to the point for mice, all the cats concluded.

"Hmmm," mulled Khaos, "I think I might like this idea, Kumplexity. You've learned much in your kitten internship! The paradoxical hiding place is great. No mouse will ever think to look there for useful information." Both Khaos and Kunfuzion secretly hoped the wise mouse leaders would hide the answer to the you-can't-have-your-cheese-and-eat-it-too paradox in one of these difficult-to-find, obvious hiding places. That was one secret they didn't want discovered.

Catching on gradually, Kunfuzion, said, "By *principles* you mean all the important insights of truth and wisdom that can help mice separate the important things from the unimportant ones, right?"

Khaos, being proud of her stepbrother's abstract comprehension improvements said, "Yes, because that is what all this creativity stuff tries to communicate in clever ways. You know, all the art, literature, and music in the mouse museums—that all tries to point the way in metaphorical terms."

At about that time Kunfuzion added, "Maybe we should also dull all mice's sensitivity and awareness of the many strange but meaningful coincidences that happen to them—like chance meetings with other mice who might be able to share their unique simple and clear truths' about how life really works and how to improve and be successful." Khaos quickly agreed.

Having a clear and simple goal and a solid plan of action, they all went off to their political contacts to finalize a proposal for a new mouse law to top cat government officials.

The proposal for the new law was already packaged so well, that it didn't need a second reading. It was straight and to the point.

Law #6: Narcosis Is the Legalized Drug of Choice.

Now Law #6 was in effect. No one could discover the important principles that could help everyone discover important things like Klarity and Simplicity...or the Plan.

This new law dulled all mice's sensitivity and kept them all from discovering any new knowledge from their individual experiences that could be generalized to other situations. They could not tune into important principles that could help them uncover the important things like Klarity and Simplicity. They were looking, but not seeing and listening, but not hearing. They would bump into walls and not even feel it.

Much truth and wisdom stayed hidden inside paradoxes. New road signs like "Ignore this sign" and "Stop and go" caused many accidents, and mouse philosopher's challenges like, "You have to lose yourself to find yourself," and "You can't have your cheese and eat it too," only resulted in more lost mice. (Khaos and Kunfuzion were most thankful for this last failure.) More valuable truth and wisdom remained totally unobserved right under mice's little twitching noses. Kumplexity's idea was pretty ingenious, and it worked well, at least for awhile.

Gradually however, all the mouse teachers started grumbling that their work was getting too difficult because they couldn't possibly teach anything meaningful if mice couldn't apply the information in a variety of other situations. After all, without general application, new knowledge was useless. And without being able to discover older important principles, past knowledge stayed hidden. "What was the purpose of education?" they all started asking.

Sensing that these feelings of discontentment might quickly spread to the general mouse population, Khaos and Kunfuzion gave up their Saturday afternoon and went off for a conflict management retreat. They invited some other cat experts to stimulate their critical thinking and creativity, two things the mice world was sorely missing. The retreat was held on the coast to allow for easier access to fresh seafood.

After a few hours, they saw progress. "I think I have the solution to our present problem," began Khaos. "We will reverse some important priorities without telling any of the mice." Anticipating the usual need of clarification for Kunfuzion, she explained, "We will start putting carts before the horses and have tails wag the dogs."

Kunfuzion was impressed and didn't need any encouragement to get started on developing some priority reversals. "Priority reversals; what an intriguing concept," he thought out loud. Actually they had already started this original confusion conspiracy with one of the better either-or afflictions—focusing on others instead of yourself. That was a priority reversal in reverse.

"The most critical priority reversal, continued Khaos, "will be flip-flopping the main task in life—fitting in and making what you are fitting into better. We will deceive mice into thinking they need to focus more on the second part, and they will spend all their precious time trying to change everything rather than first trying to understand how to fit in." Kunfuzion was extremely impressed with this devious twist his sister had conjured up. He was vaguely remembering how this might somehow be tied into the basic process of creating chaos and restoring order, but that was way too heavy for weekend thinking. The thought quickly disappeared.

This particular addition had to be subtler, and so they just slipped it in without any formality. They didn't even name it out of fear that some smart mouse might guess what was going on. It had to be something no mouse could figure out, and the fewer mice who knew about it, the better. It became a law by undeclared fiat. It was like subliminal advertising. None of the mice ever saw it coming.

There were never any questions about these new priority reversals. No mouse questioned why he had to experience failure before success, misunderstanding before understanding, or complexity before simplicity. Then there were more practical priority reversals like mice making more money toward the end of their lives instead of at the beginning when they needed it most and the mouse government spending more money on warehousing mouse criminals than on helping their victims who deserved it more.

The disorder generally went unnoticed because noticing such things was not a priority in the right order either. Besides, all the mice were too busy trying to change everything instead of trying to figure out how to fit into life. Khaos was particularly pleased since he knew the solution to the cheese paradox was safely hidden.

No mice even questioned paying kindergarten teachers much less than college professors, when young mice needed influencing the most while college students were much easier to influence. Of course, the best humorous priority reversal was making a mouse wait for dessert until last, even though it was the best part of the meal. This one was even turned into a TV ad during the mouse Super Bowl.

SUNDAY

7

Instantaneousmania

Exercising patience is like trying to idle your motor when you feel like stripping your gears.

—mouse race car driver

Sadly, as the weekend progressed, Khaos and Kunfuzion watched all their hard week's work of keeping mice confused quickly get undone. All the ultimate, special-edition mousetraps were unsprung. The whole-brained mice helped others avoid the traps of either-or dualistic thinking and mouse therapists helped self-centered egomaniacs and other unbalanced mice get more balanced. These helping professionals were even successful at helping mice put both oars in the water and more mortar between their bricks.

The mice PR agencies actively marketed the benefits of improving likability by resurrecting older virtues like patience, kindness, and tolerance. Suppressive techniques were developed to deal with unlikable characteristics like narrow-mindedness, inflexibility, and arrogance. Self-improvement became fashionable around the mouse world.

Free communication clinics helped treat various babble disorders. Mice moralists started preaching the importance of taking more responsibility for oneself. This even included taking ownership for the most bizarre, far-out behavior in their hide-and-seek games. Recognizing they were a part of whatever they were doing, was a valuable insight for mice.

Mouse colleges started offering useful courses on critical thinking to raise slipping IQ's and help mice get all the way home when the lights were on. They developed special problem-solving and conflict management seminars, and creative and intuitive thinking workshops. And finally, an especially sensitive group of mice helped others to sharpen their intuitive senses and become more sensitive to the most important things in life (such as the basic principles of how life works and how to be successful; and the meaningful coincidences that offer important clues as to who mice are, where they are going, and what they should be doing). Mice were beginning to get their act together. Klarity and Simplicity could be seen anywhere and everywhere.

Khaos and Kunfuzion knew they were headed for dire straits if they didn't do something soon. Unfortunately their creative wells were running dry, and even rational solutions weren't coming to them. By now, though, they had established a sizable organization of excellent cat thinkers and doers, and so they called an emergency weekend session with their senior cat staff. Luckily there wasn't any cat sports on TV that day, or attendance would have been light.

Their single goal for the meeting was to come up with the final solution that would divert all mice's attention from seeing, hearing, or thinking anything that might alert them to the possibility that Klarity and Simplicity were still around in the mouse world. They had to design the mousetrap of all mousetraps that could catch elephants and butterflies too. This was a tall order, but they were up to it. Maybe what they needed was to go back to the simple, classic little wooden mousetrap.

They had a number of good sales presentations at the meeting, but one stood out. It was titled: *Doing Away with Klarity and Simplicity by Speeding Up Time*. Khaos always had to add something just to feel like a contributing board member, so she proposed a brainwashing program to convince mice to resist all changes with rigorous efforts, thinking the cheese doctor's earlier instructions might be fading. Kunfuzion, being an avid Khaos supporter from the beginning and now in the position of Chief Financial Officer of their Khaotic Kunfuzion Kumpany, commented, "That seems to be a very cost-effective approach that will add substantial value to our next expenditure." "Oh brother," thought Khaos silently.

So they completed all the required paperwork processes and got the final mouse law on the books:

Law #7: There Is No More Time.

Khaos and Kunfuzion invested considerable capital in this final venture but were not at all worried. Their nap time wasn't even disrupted. This was a well conceived plan based on some solid assumptions. When all else fails, return to the basics. No questions needed to be asked. This basic mousetrap could easily be slipped in next to the more elaborate Mercedes and Rolls Royce mousetraps and go completely unnoticed. And it would contaminate most of what was already going on at the time.

Regardless of the initial cost, this seventh law was easily integrated into existing ones to produce a bigger cumulative effect. They walked away confident that they could retire from this confusion business at last. They were both ready for a very long nap. Their cat minds were getting over-worked. Besides they were working on their own time.

The impact of this new law could be felt right away. All the mice started doing things more quickly, and they all needed everything yesterday, if not sooner. Nanoseconds became eternities. Soon persevering patience was replaced by instantaneous gratification. There was no waiting for anything; aged Swiss cheese in a barrel became a thing of the past. Fast cheese drive-ins popped up everywhere, and cheese microwaves were a dime a dozen, to borrow a human phrase. There were even cheese CDs. Soon all the mice had ADHD, and there wasn't enough Ritalin to go around.

This new hyperspeed shuffle brought many changes with it, which of course were resisted by all the mice, or so they thought. Mice were moving so fast that they couldn't see the changes regardless of their illusory resistance. They were trying to resist something they were already part of, and they certainly didn't have the swimming talents of salmon who could swim upstream and climb waterfalls.

The pure centrifugal force of the merry-go-round spun off all the worthwhile and important things mice needed in order to keep up with the changes, but they were going so fast they couldn't see what was happening. Not being able to focus didn't help either. Their poor little mouse eyeballs were going round and round. Dizzy mice were dropping like flies. Change was so fast that all the mice could feel was the breeze.

The hectic pace started to bother a few mice. The bothered ones got together at a local mouse coffeehouse and started developing some time-management strategies to help slow down time. However, our friends Khaos and Kunfuzion hadn't exactly retired yet and still had a very good mouse intelligence gathering system in place. They always knew what was going on in the mouse world. Even when their eyes were closed they were still seeing. (Nobody else knows that, so please don't reveal the secret.)

Having already anticipated the possibility of would-be mice time managers, they had a new law attachment drafted ahead of time: *Everyone Must Waste Time*. It was ready to go. It didn't need an introduction. It was an automatic rebuttal. Khaos and Kunfuzion were on a roll.

Time-wasting was an easy habit to pick up. The first thing everyone did was get disorganized so nothing could be found. This wasted about 50 percent of their spare time.

They added many more clever time wasters such as never writing anything down, winging it without any kind of priority do-list, allowing uninvited interruptions all the time, and letting the boring routine things pile up. This wasted another 25 percent. They figured mice would invent their own techniques to do away with the remaining 25 percent. They were correct because, thanks to the Internet, developed earlier by one of the mouse vice-presidents, there was now high-speed connection that encouraged much on-line chatting and surfing, which was always an addicting waste of time.

The list expanded by the moment. Time-wasting was popular. Other effective time mismanagement tricks were to avoid any planning, not being accountable for results, overreacting to other mice's emergencies, and getting the urgency and importance of mouse priorities mixed up. Priorities? What were they? The wise little aphorisms of "An ounce of prevention…" and "A stitch in time" were also totally discarded from all the mouse books and mouse schools. No more planning, anticipating, or organizing.

If a mistake was made, it was fine to start all over again because that wasted a significant amount of time. Time-wasting was a misguided priority in the mouse world, but they had no idea what the word meant. Babble was still prevalent, and besides, priorities were reversed. The introduction of the habit of procrastination was delayed, but when it finally came out, what a great time waster it turned out to be. "Better late than never," said Kunfuzion observing some excellent procrastination.

What seconds were left whirled by, and mice wondered where all the time had gone. Time was flying, and nothing was getting done. All the mice were running out of time. Khaos and Kunfuzion smiled behind the scenes. They attacked their scratching post in a fit of joy. There was no need for calendars or clocks, even those things couldn't keep up with the speed of things and all this time wasting.

Mice were all traveling so fast they couldn't begin to see they had slipped back into all the bad confusion habits brought about by the previous mousetraps. They were either-oring and hiding-and-seeking again and being unlikable and miscommunicating their unthinking. They couldn't see any of this because their priorities had been reversed. Actually they couldn't see anything because they were traveling at the speed of light.

The two cat leaders' work was finally done, and they still had a few hours of their weekend left to eat, play, or nap, whichever they fancied most. To say they were pleased was an understatement.

Conclusion to Part I

> *If you have anything to tell me of importance, for goodness sake, begin at the end.*
>
> —anonymous mouse

Being too successful can be a problem. It can get boring. Even being in control can get boring. Late Sunday evening Khaos looked at Kunfuzion and said woefully, "You know Kunfuzion, we need a change for next week."

Kunfuzion, having gotten much smarter over the week, saw what was coming. "Yes, Khaos, I know what you mean. Life is too easy and we are all getting bored. We need a challenge."

Being armed with all the knowledge from their law-making experiences in high-tech mousetrap design and now in need of developing a new challenge, the two set out to rediscover where they had hidden Klarity and Simplicity. But first they had to have a plan and set some measurable goals. They held their last meeting.

After a few hours of using all the skills that they had outlawed in the mice world, they decided on a simple and clear solution. They needed to pass one more final law: All these other laws needed to be reversed by wording them positively. The best way to achieve total and lasting confusion is to tell the truth clearly and simply. Nobody ever believes it that way. The cats momentarily pondered the possibility that this might be their own ultimate hide-and-seek game but let the idea go because they had other things to do.

This last truth scheme didn't take long to catch on because by now both mice and cats were getting tired of all this mousetrap mayhem. There were too many headaches and not enough aspirin. They all wanted Klarity and Simplicity desperately. There were joint demonstrations, and the noisy crowds were chanting, "We want Klarity and Simplicity!"

So the final undoing law was passed unanimously by both cats and mice: *All the Other Laws Are Hereby Reversed*.

There was a huge celebration with a ticker-tape parade. Everyone was encouraged to join the search for Klarity and Simplicity using any means they could. The "how" wasn't important, only results. They were instructed to remember what they had forgotten. Anything was a go. Even discovering *how to have your cheese and eat it too* was no longer tabooed. Now mice could listen and talk plainly, even to cats. The brighter ones could even learn the human language. They could think about their unthinking and communicate about their miscommunication. They became amazed at all the clarity and simplicity this change revealed.

They could think critically, be likable, pay attention to their intuition, and experiment with creativity. The new positive thinking, practice of inclusion, and application of critical "P" points all caught hold again, only this time for good. They could get what they wanted and needed by being assertive. Simple things became more enjoyable, because they were slowing down and more able to enjoy what they had. They saw that they needed to first learn how to fit into what they were a part of and then make changes from the inside-out. It helped greatly that they could finally see what they were looking at.

The mice could take on the challenges of solving problems and resolving conflicts and not worry too much about making mistakes. They practiced both rational and creative problem-solving techniques to separate real problems from symptoms and analyze the best solutions. With conflicts they learned to study all the issues that were involved, what investments were already made, and what the cost of implementing various alternative resolutions would be. The mice finally started seeing the connections between things.

Dependable definitions returned to words and mice worked hard at clarifying misunderstanding, especially in the area of verifying interpretations of non-verbal behavior. They grew exponentially by the minute. They even became aware of all their thoughts and feelings and knew the difference between the two. The cats were most impressed with this last mouse achievement.

The entire mouse world started viewing failure as a temporary setback rather than a permanent condition. Lost cheese could be replaced with found liver pate. "Don't worry, be happy" was a frequent verbal greeting. They developed mistake recovery strategies so they didn't have to avoid any risky behavior that might result in mistakes.

By owning their own mistakes, apologizing, implementing quick fixes, and developing long-range cures to keep the problems from re-occurring, they were easily forgiven for even the worst of mistakes they made. They knew they were bound to make some mistakes, but they also realized that they weren't bound to the mistakes they made (Kunfuzion, the aspiring philosopher, slipped this in at the last minute).

The mice even stopped assuming too much and started asking good questions. They began to question their most sacred viewpoints, such as aged Swiss being better than Pimento. They began to plan their questions better to get more complete and accurate information. Questions such as "Where is my cheese?" were rephrased as "Has anyone seen the thing for which I have been searching or any other reasonable substitute that might interest me? They avoided asking questions that led to deceitful and partial information, like "Why did you take my cheese?" And they stopped asking open-ended questions that produced rambling answers that had no end like, "Tell me about your cheese."

Mice understood the need to get more balanced. Now there were ham-and-cheese sandwiches, work and play, and talking and listening. They paid equal attention to themselves and other mice. A sense of mouse "oneness" was becoming a common peak experience, while division and alienation were falling by the wayside. More lasting glimpses of Klarity and Simplicity quickly became the norm. Order was being restored. The picture was getting sharper and clearer; DVD and Surround Sound were introduced in the mouse world. No more cracked mouse glasses, dizzy mice, or mouse mental hospitals.

Mice finally began to see and do what was most important. They got their priorities straight: cheese carts followed horses, and tails no longer wagged dogs. They now knew what the word "priority" meant. They were fitting in and learning how to eat part of their cheese and still have some left over. Best of all, mice could start paying closer attention to their real self and discover why they had unthinkingly allowed themselves to become tricked by two mischievous Siamese cats, Khaos and Kunfuzion. The song, "How Stupid I Was" stayed number one on the music charts for a whole year. It even became the all-time top movie at the box office, replacing both "Gone with the Wind" and "Star Wars."

Mice finally started noticing the gaps between where they were and where they wanted to be. They became skilled at seeing the gaps between how they saw themselves and how others saw them and who they pretended to be and who they actually where. They started becoming self-actualized in walking their talk. They made genuine efforts to continually improve themselves and took full responsibility for their actions. In their humility they became quite likable. They also had more cheese than they knew what to do with.

A few hours after these last efforts were completed, Klarity and Simplicity were sitting around enjoying their success and peace of mind and engaging in friendly conversation. "By the way," Klarity said to Simplicity, "Where did Khaos and Kunfuzion go?"

Simplicity just winked at Klarity. Klarity understood and whispered back, "This was too much work. It was very entertaining, but I am exhausted. I think I am enjoying things more this way. Let's not talk about it anymore, at least for this week."

In their dreams that night, the two tired mice both dreamt about all the endless varieties of this conspiracy plan of which they had just taken part. They smiled contently in their sleep, being vividly assured that life would never get too dull or become a boring routine. There would always be plenty of stimulating challenges no matter who was trying to create chaos or restore order. Complicated, confusing chaos would always require some clarification and simplification. The resulting order, of course, would always have to be mixed up with some more chaos for the sake of interest, excitement, and adventure. The secrecy of this ultimate conspiracy was still intact.

PART II

The Solution

Heal the past, live in the present, dream of the future.
—Mary Engelbreit

What the two mouse leaders, Klarity and Simplicity, didn't realize was that it was just "halftime." Both cats and mice have two distinct halves of their lives. The first half is devoted to creating chaos by spreading gaps between where they are and where they want to be. The second half is spent restoring order by closing these gaps. In a sense, the first half of life is a challenge to discover what the problems are, while the second half is a challenge to figure out how to apply the cure. Of course, all cats and mice are trying to do both of these things during the first half of their lives and not doing either very well. Hence the popular saying, "You can't have your cheese and eat it too."

During halftime, there is a major change in viewpoints for all cats and mice. There is a shift from chasing "cheese" in order to control life and make it into what they want, to understanding life and accepting it for what it is. During halftime cats, mice, and even people finally start to find out who they are, where they are going, and how to have their cheese and eat it too.

Khaos and Kunfuzion's new adoptive parent, Doc, having made this transition himself earlier, wrote an article on the matter for a widely read human personal development magazine, *Personal Excellence*. He described a few key "symptoms" that characterize the critical shift: moving from an outside focus to an inside one, exchanging the role of being a teacher back to being a student, and noticing the connection between your actions and their consequences. The biggest gains could be found in realizing the power of choice in each new moment and tapping into "P" Point creative solutions to life's problems. He left the article out for the two cats to read at their leisure along side of some tasty hairball treatment treats.

After digesting the article's meaning and the treats, Khaos and Kunfuzion decided to go off by themselves to apply all the wisdom they had gained during the first half of their lives. They had learned much from this fun exercise with the mouse leaders. After a few weeks by themselves, the two cats decided to form an unconventional domestic partnership and begin a family of their own. They were planning for some little kittens to join them soon and were excited about the prospects of becoming cat parents. After all, they needed some challenges.

Actually they had now been adopted by two human "parents" who themselves were in a domestic partnership, which gave Khaos and Kunfuzion the idea. They lived with Doc and Toots near a college town on a quiet lake in the middle of the country. Summers were hot and humid, and winters were cold and snowy.

During the transition to the second half of life, things started to become simpler and clearer. Their field of vision became less cluttered and better focused. Now Khaos and Kunfuzion could easily see the most important things they needed to do and also the things they needed to avoid. They could even see how to do all these things easier and more effectively, especially closing the gap between where they were and where they wanted to be. The 1,000-mph, whirlwind chaos was becoming a sea of calm. Their top priority was to pass on this new wisdom to their family-to-be. That was the right thing to do, and they had a pretty good idea of the right way to do it.

Being smart cats, they thought it would be a good idea to develop a parenting plan ahead of time. Their main idea was to teach their kittens how to have a head, heart, and hands team. This is what every cat needs to become whole—smart thinking, sensitive feeling, and the right behavior. They could accomplish this by developing a list of simple suggestions of do's and don'ts that would help their kittens develop genuine spiritual power and guide them to prosperity, success, and happiness in their lives. They would encourage their kittens to focus first on fitting in instead of wasting so much time trying to change things they didn't yet understand. This was the ultimate solution to the perplexing paradox of how to have your cheese and eat it too, which they had discovered from the earlier Master Mental Mousetrap Plan.

Their own parents had done something similar with them, only they never organized a formal list or put a name on the important lessons they taught them. Their parents were from the old cat world and didn't have any formal education. They always knew what they were doing, but just didn't have a fancy name for it. Times were changing, as Khaos and Kunfuzion realized.

So one rainy weekend the two would-be parents got together to start working on their project. First they brainstormed all the important things their own parents had taught them. They came up with a list of about 50 things. They both wanted to keep this as simple as they could and quickly decided to divide the list into do's and don'ts, with suggestions for each.

Besides the fact that Khaos was always hung up with dividing things into opposite categories, she also had a thing about the number 10. But this time Kunfuzion was going to have his say. After some thoughtful rewording, creative combining of items from the original list, and minor negotiation, the two cats agreed upon 10 simple do's and nine even simpler don't suggestions to give to their kittens.

For the next few hours the two cats worked diligently to make sure they hadn't forgotten anything really important and to be certain they were communicating their ideas clearly and simply. This project was too important to risk poor communication. Here is how the list turned out:

Do's

1. Dream Big.
2. Listen Carefully.
3. Enjoy Everything.
4. Be Positive.
5. Get Smart.
6. Be Reverent.
7. Laugh Often.
8. Get Involved.
9. Use Your Talents.
10. Improve and Grow.

Don'ts

1. Don't Hurry.
2. Don't Quit.
3. Don't Lie.
4. Don't Be Dishonest.
5. Don't Gossip.
6. Don't Be Irresponsible.
7. Don't Judge.
8. Don't Worry.
9. Don't Wander.

Khaos beamed, "I think this is really a good, simple list of suggestions for our kittens. This will help them to be happy and successful."

"I agree," chimed in Kunfuzion, but then added, "now comes the hard work."

"What do you mean?" asked a slightly puzzled Khaos.

"Well," began Kunfuzion, "We need to carefully explain these things in just the right amount of detail and then tell why they are so important and maybe figure out how they can be taught best. We might even have to anticipate some questions our kittens might want to ask, based on our own earlier experiences as kittens."

"I see what you mean by hard work," concluded Khaos. Her suggestion was to go have a catnap and dream on this matter. Long catnaps are always good for coming up with good ideas. Plus they are always good for getting some sleep.

Visions of slow running, plump mice already filled Khaos's mischievous cat mind. Kunfuzion preferred to dream about sunny beaches in the Pacific and romantic meals at big city gourmet cat restaurants. Grilled Mahi Mahi with fresh rice pilaf was his favorite entrée. Khaos savored key lime cheesecake.

The last thing Kunfuzion usually heard before dozing off was Khaos licking her lips. Sometimes she was especially noisy doing this, which annoyed Kunfuzion slightly, but fortunately he was tolerant of his stepsister's minor foibles. That made for a smoother relationship.

So off the two Siamese cats went to their favorite napping location—their human owner's bed. Kunfuzion's spot was between the pillows, while Khaos took the middle of the bed. They took about a two-hour, forty-three-minute nap. That was about their normal nap duration on a rainy weekday, which this was. Naps were even longer when the sun was shinning just right. Then of course, naps by the fireplace on a cold winter's weekend could be all-dayers.

The cats awoke slowly and moseyed out to their food bowls where some fresh salmon was waiting for them. Their two owners, Doc and Toots, took great care of them, although they didn't particularly like the term "owners." They were part of the family, and nobody owned anyone. Doc and Toots were domestic partners and Khaos and Kunfuzion were their "kids." Soon Khaos and Kunfuzion would learn what that meant for themselves.

Doc and Toots had some suspicions as to what the two cats might be up to, so they wanted to make sure they had some good food for thought. They were both very loving people themselves and took great delight in what their two cats were about to do. They even left some good self-development reading material around to help stimulate discussion, even the mouse doctor's book, *Who Moved My Cheese?* Occasionally Doc left the TV on when a good family-values show was playing. No violent TV shows in this household, and no silly reality TV.

CHAPTER 8

The Do List

The more things are forbidden,
the more popular they become.
—famous cat rebel

Khaos and Kunfuzion were positive-minded cats so they wanted to start things out by offering their kittens some suggestions for what they should do in order to get the most fun, happiness, and success out of life.

Most of the other cat world rules spelled out the things you couldn't or shouldn't do, especially the ones handed down by the humans. So Khaos and Kunfuzion were eager to get going with their positive do list. These were the things they thought everyone should do, especially their kittens. By doing these things themselves, Khaos and Kunfuzion found happiness, wisdom, and contentment and avoided much unnecessary anger, failure, and unhappiness.

Do Suggestion #1: Dream Big.

> *All my life I always wanted to be somebody. Now I realize that I should have been more specific.*
>
> —Jane Wagner, daydreamer

Khaos was the first to speak, " If there is one thing I have learned that I think is really important, it is to dream BIG. Look at us. We had dreams of living in a big nice house by a lake so we could look at all the birds and have a dozen different napping places, all on one floor. We preferred educated, affectionate, fun-loving owners who understood our need for independence, lots of sleep time, and superb chow and who weren't neurotic about having cat hair all over their clothes and furniture."

We also knew we needed good care from a reputable veterinarian and nice new cars in which to drive there. And we wished for a basement or attic that might have an occasional mouse running around."

"Just think Kunfuzion, we got all this plus a lot more. On top of all this good fortune, we even have a book being written about us," concluded Khaos proudly. She kept to herself her dream about a movie. Khaos was an incurable big-time dreamer who even fantasized about winning Feline Powerball. "Believe and Receive" was her silent motto.

"Yes," said Kunfuzion, "we shouldn't be afraid of having big dreams. After all, if you believe in something, it is more likely to happen." "Actually, anything you can believe can happen," he pointed out. Kunfuzion remembered all the early comic books he used to read about spaceships and then the eventual space travel that became a reality.

Kunfuzion was the practical one who anticipated the "yes, but..." question. He wisely warned, "Just having big dreams is only a start. Just like this simple list of suggestions, we have to work hard at making this dream a useful reality for our kittens by explaining everything in easy-to-understand and practical terms, which isn't always easy." Khaos caught on quickly and added the "but" part, "Dream big, but understand that you have to do something to make your dreams come true. Sometimes this requires cleverness and hard work, because things don't just happen by magic."

The two cats both remembered suffering through their miserable birthplace, fighting the cold, lizards, dogs, birds, flees, ear mites, cardboard-box beds, unappetizing dry cat food, and 50 other cats. Life back then was pretty dismal.

When the two prospective adoptive parent's Doc and Toots, came to check them out one cold winter night, they both put on their charm and affection, which sealed the deal. They tried hard to be likable and irresistible, and they were. What they didn't realize was that Doc and Toots had only planned to get one cat.

When the two cats got to their new dream home, they appreciated it and showed their appreciation to Doc and Toots. They were happy and successful in making their dreams come true and showed their appreciation by being content and occasionally entertaining visiting guests. Of course, they knew that focusing on fitting in before going wild trying to change everything allowed their dreams to come true.

Not wanting to be too superficial in explaining this first suggestion, Khaos had some more to say. She reminded her stepbrother, Kunfuzion, that they were both very different cats. She was big, calm and wise, while Kunfuzion was small, hyper, and a little mentally disjointed. She loved to lie on Doc and Toots and watch birds, and Kunfuzion loved to eat and play on the scratching post, even though he had already been de-clawed. She was majestically beautiful, and Kunfuzion was just cute.

But they both believed in themselves enough to be confident in becoming unconventional domestic partners/parents despite their differences and a few unsuccessful relationships along the way that had them both questioning their worth. They had also learned valuable wisdom from their earlier activities with the mice. They didn't want to be reminded of how dazed and confused they both got from all the chaos and gap spreading that had gone on.

Khaos and Kunfuzion both realized that it was their own parents who had helped them have a healthy dose of self-confidence, mainly by teaching them these other important suggestions and having patience with them. They both secretly wished that their kittens would be smart enough to see the connections between all these things from the beginning, but they knew it would never be that easy. They had recently learned that secret for themselves. Their own dreams were just now starting to come true.

The two cats decided how they would teach this value of dreaming big to their kittens. They would research a list of great and inspiring cat heroes and then leave a few of their biographies lying around the house to motivate the kittens. They would also communicate what they were doing to the school where they would be sending their kittens in order to reinforce this idea. From their own experiences, they realized there really wasn't enough good communication between parents and schools about basic values. Sometimes they would each be teaching things that were at odds with the other.

Values are things that need to be discussed carefully and understood fully, because they drive behavior. It was good for Khaos and Kunfuzion to be in agreement about something as important as core values. They had learned that lack of agreement was often just a result of poor communication and misunderstanding.

This last discussion brought up a pressing concern with Khaos, and she had not yet figured out what to do about it. She was concerned with the growing consciousness of cats beyond the everyday activities of eating, playing, and sleeping. She sensed from her own experience that other cats were starting to think about higher, spiritual matters. Routine cat activities were becoming less important. Cat schools strayed away from this delicate subject, but it might be time to reconsider a more intimate relationship between teachers and parents about spiritual subjects.

Both cats knew this wouldn't be easy, but sooner or later it couldn't be avoided. They trusted that when the time came, they would know how to do it. Right now they had a project they were working on, and they couldn't get too far ahead of themselves...or they wouldn't do a good job.

Do Suggestion #2: Listen Carefully.

> *One of the best ways to persuade others is to listen to them.*
>
> —Dean Rusk

Kunfuzion admitted, "This is the one I had most trouble with myself. I wish I had listened to my parents about the importance of listening instead of talking so much. They told me that if God wanted us to talk more and listen less, He would have given us two mouths and just one ear." Khaos gloated a bit, realizing most of her wisdom had come from good listening. But she also realized she wasn't born with hyperactivity and didn't have a clue what that was like.

Regardless, both cats instantly recognized that they were both guilty of failing to listen to their parents. "Why is it we don't give our parents any credit for all they know?" thought both cats out loud. Then it quickly came to them: Maybe their parents didn't listen to them enough.

Kunfuzion had gotten smarter over the past few months and realized there were lots of important things worth listening to. He started listening to his inner voice, his conscience, his intuition, the clues about how life really worked, and the important advice older people gave. As a result he started learning how to be more likable, happier, and more successful at things he was trying to do. Now he had more answers than questions. All he had to do was listen carefully, with both ears. Talk once, listen twice was the rule.

Kunfuzion also learned that people would listen to him much more when he wasn't talking so much. When he was a little kitten, he meowed so much that nobody ever heard what he was trying to say. Needless to say, he was ignored, and he didn't know what to do to get attention. That is when all the crazy behavior began; little kittens will say or do anything to get attention. Then it becomes a hard habit to stop, even when all you are getting is negative attention. Any kind of attention is addictive—the more you get the more you want.

Khaos always saw connections between things, and that was why she had so much difficulty limiting these suggestions to just 10. She wanted to make sure their little kittens knew that talking and listening were just two of the many areas cats should try to keep balanced, and that balance was a related area of concern.

Anytime you get out of balance, you can easily step into a mousetrap, which was the ultimate humiliation in the cat world. Khaos's advice was, "Listen to learn new things and talk to learn them better." Kunfuzion saw a slightly different application: "Get in the middle and then you can see in both directions. That gives you more running room." This was just one of many ways that Khaos and Kunfuzion could look at the same thing and come up with two entirely different, but correct and useful interpretations.

Kunfuzion had special difficulty trying to determine whether to listen to his head or heart. Eventually he figured out that they speak about the same thing but in different languages and that when these two things disagree you need to listen more closely to where that disagreement comes from.

Resolving head-and-heart conflicts was indeed a difficult task, reflected Kunfuzion. Of course, the wise Khaos purred silently, knowing very well that head and heart babble is only worth listening to when they both agree. That insight didn't come easily though. There had been plenty of heartaches along the way.

For instance, when your heart loves somebody and your head finds all kinds of logical shortcomings that warn you off, which do you listen to? Khaos and Kunfuzion knew that true love didn't have that conflict. They had both made mistakes following the feelings of their hearts, only to realize that wasn't enough. They concluded that their brains had valuable information worth knowing. Maybe the key was to tune into their intuition walkie-talkies, which are valuable links between the head and heart.

The ideas of listening and sensitivity reminded Kunfuzion of something else extremely important to pass on to their kittens. This was being more sensitive and listening closer for the subtle but meaningful coincidences that could help them understand something important. Kunfuzion assumed Khaos would just know what he meant, which she did. They both experienced these strange sorts of coincidences.

Khaos had some last-minute advice concerning listening skills. "When you are dealing with other cats, you need to resist your temptation to dwell too much on *how* some cats say things. You miss *what* they are trying to say, which is really more important."

"Remember, you can say "yes" and not really mean it, or be mean and hateful in your words and really just be hurting yourself on the inside." "Also," she continued, "try to listen to really understand what the other cat is saying rather than just listening enough to offer a clever response. When you listen to understand, you can learn a lot of valuable information you can use later."

Not knowing when she was going past the point of perfection, Khaos kept rambling, "Sometimes when you listen more carefully, you will learn the best thing to say in return."

Kunfuzion thought this was getting a bit too deep, so he suggested they go take a nap for a few hours. Off they went, this time to the computer room, which had two comfortable matching chairs. This was one of their earlier dreams—to have matching sleeping chairs and a Microsoft mouse to watch out of the corner of their eye. They also had fun visiting all the cat sites on the Internet when Doc and Toots were at work. What they wanted was an e-mail account.

Do Suggestion #3: Enjoy Everything.

> *The way I see it, if you want the rainbow, you gotta put up with the rain.*
>
> —Dolly Parton

This suggestion was one of Kunfuzion's main contributions. When younger, he was on the hyperactive side and so had the habit of rushing from one thing to another, without ever enjoying any one thing for very long.

After many years of missing out on so much enjoyment, he finally wised up to the importance of paying more attention to what he had right in front of him before it was gone. He also finally woke up to the fact that the food wasn't always better in the other cat's bowl. Sometimes it was just a different brand of yucky dry cat food.

Even though Khaos was pretty smart about learning how to want what she already had instead of always wanting what she didn't, she still thought this suggestion was a good one for their kittens to learn. She remarked, "It is often the little ordinary things right in front of you that are of most value." "Real wealth," she continued, "is when you get great pleasure and enjoyment from free things, like watching sunsets, dreaming about catching birds, or walking leisurely outside in deep green grass."

Kunfuzion admired his stepsister's ability to get so much enjoyment out of such simple things. Khaos' enjoyment actually increased his own enjoyment. Khaos thought to herself, "Now he's catching on, I hope this is as easy when we have to start teaching our kittens." Eventually she would remember that this was one of those things you just had to demonstrate firsthand, rather than talk about.

Khaos also knew something else really important but didn't quite know how to say it clearly and simply, because it was somewhat of an intellectual concept that might be too high in the sky for normal minds. Sensing this concern, Kunfuzion, tried to help out. "Maybe what you are trying to get across," he started, "is that it is not very smart to automatically divide everything into opposite groups like good versus bad, okay versus not okay, right versus wrong, pretty versus ugly, and so on." Both had conveniently overlooked that they had done this with their do versus don't list. "Oh well, maybe there are some times when this is acceptable," rationalized Khaos.

Khaos continued, "When you do this all the time you are really just cutting your fun and happiness in half." "Yes," commented Khaos, "that's what I mean, but how do you explain how we can stop doing that when it seems so natural?"

Neither cat had a good answer to that perplexing question, but they did remember some things they had overheard Doc discussing with Toots. (Please don't reveal this cat ability to understand humans; another fact that is generally not known.) Doc had said that we all have to first realize how we prejudge things and needlessly limit our possibilities for fun and enjoyment. We have to understand that we are just cheating ourselves by doing this.

The cats made a promise that they would always demonstrate the knack of seeing some good in everything that might seem bad and showing how something might be okay in some situations but not in others.

This would have to be something they would show rather than talk about, as they were already getting confused about what they were trying to say. It was definitely time for a nap. Too much strenuous thinking was hard on cats.

Do Suggestion #4: Be Positive.

> *Things turn out best for cats who make the best of how things turn out.*
>
> —enlightened cat philosopher

Both Khaos and Kunfuzion were very positive cats. That is why they were such good partners and so successful in what they did. They couldn't imagine why anyone would ever be negative. It didn't make any sense. But of course they had two parents who were both positive, and Doc and Toots were another positive pair.

Being realistic though, both cats realized that it was easy to have a positive attitude when things were going well, but more difficult when things weren't going so well. This was when a positive attitude counted most. Practicing having a positive attitude under normal circumstances helped a little. The more you practice something, the more it is available when you really need it the most. Khaos remembered her own father's advice: "When you are down, a negative attitude will take you lower, but a positive attitude will move you higher."

Khaos and Kunfuzion decided they would teach this important value with a few stories. One story they particularly liked was the one about a human's daughter who came crying to her father one day. She was depressed and frustrated and wanted to give up on life. Life was too hard on her. The father, who was a chef, got out three pots, put in some water and turned on the stove.

He placed some eggs in the first, some carrots in the second, and some coffee grounds in the third one. After they were boiled he took the eggs, carrots, and coffee out and asked his daughter what she saw. "Carrots, eggs, and coffee," was her quick reply.

"No," her father said, "There is more to it than that. We put hard, strong carrots in the boiling water, and they came out soft and weak. With the eggs, they were fragile and delicate going into the boiling water and came out hard. When we put the coffee into the boiling water, it made something entirely new out of the water. If boiling water is your adversity, will you be the carrot, the egg, or the coffee?"

Needless to say, the daughter learned something important that day.

There was one thing about having a positive attitude that really appealed to Khaos and Kunfuzion: It didn't cost anything. It was completely free. They had always thought, "Why in the world wouldn't every cat take advantage of such a wonderful thing?"

Then they became humble when they remembered what it is like to get your heart broken or not make the basketball team or cheerleader squad at school. They also got to see Doc and Toots apply their own best advice when Doc didn't have a job and they were low on money. That was when a positive attitude really helped. It would have been easy to be a sour puss then.

Right before going off for another nap, Khaos recalled an interesting explanation for negative, pessimistic cats, which she had read in one of her cat magazines. Such a cat's sole purpose was to serve as a warning for others. "Ha Ha," they both laughed before closing their eyes.

Do Suggestion #5: Get Smart.

> *What you think you know may not always be so.*
>
> —Doc

Khaos and Kunfuzion had both studied the notion of intelligence extensively and realized it was much misunderstood. They were both teachers now, trying to teach intelligence, but many of their early failures were because they didn't know how to learn and teach intelligently. "Odd," they both concluded, "that we go to school to learn before we are taught how to learn properly."

The two cats knew that being smart is much more than having a high IQ, knowing lots of information, and being quick to answer questions. Khaos once gave her students a good definition of getting smart. "Getting smart," she lectured, "is learning how to start doing the right things in the right way to get the right results for the right reasons." Most of the students thought there were so many "rights" in the definition that it had to be right. To balance things out, she then added, "More than anything, getting smart is being able to admit to yourself when that isn't happening."

Over the months the two cats learned the difference between information and knowledge. Information is what you get from memorizing details, like the parts of your body. On the other hand, knowledge is the understanding you gain when you study how all these things work together so you can fix them when they get broken.

Khaos and Kunfuzion remembered some of the important signs they were given to let them know they were getting smart. First, they began questioning things they had previously just assumed to be true. Then they started realizing how little they actually knew and just how much more there was to learn.

With this humble but accurate realization, they learned how to focus on asking good questions rather than using old answers nobody wanted to hear. In turn, they were able to see relationships between things, opportunities for making choices, and the advantage of seeing the probable consequences of making those choices. Finally they learned how to start accumulating genuine power by making the right choices and avoiding the wrong ones. This was the process of getting smart.

In looking back on the process of getting smart, both Khaos and Kunfuzion could see that, just like writing a book, there is always a start, middle, and conclusion. They started getting smart by doing little things, such as asking questions, listening to what others had to say, and learning what mistakes they were making.

Then they started to apply what they were learning to more important things like getting balanced, separating what they thought they wanted from what they actually needed, and practicing all these do-and-don't suggestions themselves instead of imposing them on others.

Finally, they started to put everything back together again that they had taken apart earlier. This involved helping others feel the power of the most important things they had learned from getting smart: love, compassion, understanding, and knowledge.

Khaos and Kunfuzion knew that getting smart is really nothing more than knowing how to close the gap between where you are and where you want to be. There is no set prescription on how to do that, but rather, unlimited possibilities. They thought this was the best possible gift from life—a truly equal opportunity for everyone and everything. This was a good way to reach a conclusion about getting smart: The opportunity is there for everyone.

Kunfuzion learned one particular thing about getting smart that he wanted to share with his kittens. When you take the normal, conventional perception of time out of the equation, concentrate more on the here and now, and begin to see how the past and future are both just an extension of now, there seems to be much more time to do all the things that help you get smart. Besides, he never did like timed tests in school. They kept some cats from showing how smart they really were.

Khaos thought it would be helpful if she concluded this particular suggestion with a good example of being smart. "When you say something nice to someone else and they aren't asking for it, do it in private or public according to their preference. Have no ulterior motive in doing this, and don't expect anything in return. If it helps the cat have a better day than he started out with and he manages to turn around and do something good for another cat during the day, you are being smart."

Do Suggestion #6: Be Reverent.

> *Walk lightly in the spring, for Mother Nature is pregnant.*
>
> —Native American saying

Of course, Kunfuzion just had to ask the question, "What is reverence?" Khaos, who always liked to use new and unusual words, was glad her partner had asked this question. That was always her favorite way of starting something off—by using a key word and then defining precisely what it meant for everyone to get started in exactly the same place in their understanding of what was to follow. She had learned this technique from one of her favorite teachers. She had also just learned something even more important: it means more to show people what something like "smartness" is than to tell them how to get it, or worse yet, to let them know they don't have it.

Khaos' answer to the present question was short and to the point, because that was the best way to communicate. She simply said, "Being reverent is showing polite respect for everyone and everything on this planet." This was easy enough for Kunfuzion to understand. He had wrongly anticipated an explanation based on religion.

Kunfuzion asked Khaos, "This seems pretty reasonable, so why wouldn't everyone, including people, act this way naturally?" Khaos began what was to be a long-winded speech, "Most people—and even some cats—get so caught up in their own self-importance and are so busy in their own worlds that they forget they are only a small part of the whole universe.

"We are all really just guests here on earth and we should respect each other and be polite to one another. But of course humans tend to think they are far superior to everything else around them. Even us cats think we are better than mice, don't we? Humans are more advanced than monkeys and dolphins, and then of course bugs and twigs and rocks are even further down on the food chain than we are. But the point is that humans were given brains so they can take care of the rest of us, which they obviously aren't doing very well."

"I think if we could do away with making lists of highest to lowest, we might lick this problem," offered Kunfuzion. "For instance in this list of suggestions, everything is equally important and equally valuable. No one suggestion is better than another. They all come together to get your head, heart, and hands working together as a team."

Khaos interjected, "That produces genuine spiritual power and makes a cat whole, leading to real happiness, success, and contentment. This is the only way to have your cheese and eat it too."

Khaos took a breather and thought about how her own personal habit of staring up at the stars at least once a week helped her to remember how small she was and to learn this important lesson about humility and reverence. It helped her better understand how she fit in. She could enjoy looking at the stars, and they could enjoy being seen. No words were needed.

"Why is being reverent so important?" asked Kunfuzion, bringing his partner back to reality. Khaos was quick to reply, "Because being reverent is putting the Golden Rule into practice, and this is a simple, clear guideline for everyone to follow. It really summarizes all the rest." She continued, "I know you remember that the Golden Rule teaches us to treat all the other cats just like we want to be treated ourselves. How can anything be any clearer or easier?

"Personally I think we need to extend this rule to include everything. After all, we all want to be respected, treated with fairness, nurtured, loved, listened to, and valued, even the trees, spiders, and those darned mice."

Seeing things clearly and simply, Kunfuzion said, "It seems to me that if we are going to teach our kittens what is important, then we can just teach them the Golden Rule. That rule answers every possible question they could ever have about how they need to be or what they need to do."

"I can't argue with that conclusion," remarked Khaos, "but we still have some other advice worth giving, don't we?"

"Yes," said Kunfuzion, "I certainly want our kittens to develop a good sense of humor, as you helped me do." The words were barely out of his mouth when they both realized that this was putting the Golden Rule into practice.

Do Suggestion #7: Laugh Often.

> *Laughing is as necessary for your heart as loving is for your soul and exercising is for your body.*
>
> —Khaos

Kunfuzion knew his stepsister had a great sense of humor and appreciated how she helped him to loosen up and laugh more. Laughing was good medicine for the whole world. Therefore, he could see the value of passing this suggestion on to their kittens.

After all, there are only a few tragedies in life at which you can't laugh. Just like having a positive attitude to help you get out of a negative situation, taking the time to see something funny about a serious situation can make it less serious. Khaos's words, "Don't take life too seriously because you're not going to get out of it alive," had always made an impression on him.

"I guess the trick'" Khaos said, "is to have plenty of things around to make you laugh. I keep some funny pictures of myself handy when I figure I am taking myself too seriously. Remember that one of me when I was cross-eyed and was doing Halloween cat with a fat tail?"

"Yes," replied Kunfuzion, "and do you remember that one of me standing on Toot's daughter Susan's shoulder?" They both started laughing when Khaos brought up the many pictures Doc had taken of them both sleeping upside down and sideways twisted like pretzels. You couldn't tell where Khaos ended and Kunfuzion started.

"And when I am giving a talk at a cat convention," Kunfuzion interjected, "I like to tell jokes as a way to make a serious point. When you can get people laughing about themselves and some of the silly and stupid ways they keep themselves from getting somewhere, you have removed a major barrier."

This was getting a bit too academic even for Khaos. She quickly advised, "Maybe we should just make a pledge to take our kittens to the zoo once or twice a year. Some of the other animals are so funny, especially with the humans watching them. You can't tell who is entertaining who with the monkeys and humans. A trip to the zoo is always a way to appreciate God's own grand sense of humor." Kunfuzion couldn't have agreed more.

The two prospective cat parents decided that right then and there they would set aside an hour every Friday night for telling cat jokes. They might even have joke parties for some of the other cats in the neighborhood. The only requirements would be the ability to laugh loudly and bring a good joke or two. The two parents-to-be were quickly realizing that this little exercise they were engaging in for their kittens was just as much help to them too. They were learning about themselves and their own values.

Being psychologically trained, Khaos already knew that you had to change something about yourself before you could help someone else change. In the same sense, you can't teach something without learning at the same time. They were beginning to see the give and take in their do-and-don't suggestions. Maybe their kittens would have some good suggestions for them too. They promised to listen and be open to that distinct possibility.

Do Suggestion #8: Get Involved.

> *Tell me and I'll forget. Show me and I may not remember. Involve me and I'll understand.*
>
> —Native American saying

Khaos had been an activist in her early days as a kitten, but somehow she lost her drive to get involved in anything but her writing and teaching. Thank heavens for Kunfuzion's spirit of involvement to help her go from the sidelines into the game again. She was starting to feel as though something was lacking without knowing what.

Kunfuzion knew very well that most of life's fun, excitement, pleasure, and satisfaction comes from getting involved in worthwhile activities. The two cats had already agreed to do everything they could to encourage their kittens to get into the habit of being involved in a variety of school, church, and community activities. If it meant cutting into their own free time or leaving work early to provide transportation, then so be it. Whatever effort it took, it would be worth it.

"So what practical benefits did we experience from getting involved?" asked Kunfuzion. Khaos replied, "It is fun and exciting to participate in activities at school or in the community or anywhere. And of course, you always learn important lessons about life from your involvement in activities."

"Don't you remember how much fun we had collecting canned goods for the food pantry and washing people's cars for free during Lent and how we then understood what the priest meant by 'charity' and 'penitence.'" "Ah, yes," fondly recalled Kunfuzion, "but sometimes I get so involved in things that I forget how much fun I am having or what I am actually learning, such as the time we wrote our congressmen about political issues."

Khaos wasn't interested in politics so she quickly changed the subject to the importance of cats using their talents.

Do Suggestion #9: Use Your Talents.

Life without you would be like a broken pencil. Completely pointless.
—Khaos' mother

The importance of cats using their talents was something close to Khaos' little cat heart. Her father dedicated a stained glass window at their church with a reference to the Bible story about the parable of the talents, to Mrs. Khaos' loving memory. This Bible story told of a father who gave his three sons five, two, and one talent respectively. The son given five talents returned with ten, the son given two talents returned with four, while the son given one talent only returned with the same one because he had buried it, thinking it was more valuable that way. He ended up with no talents. His brothers flourished. He didn't. The moral lesson: Use your talents.

Khaos once told Kunfuzion that before we were born, all of us made a secret contract with God and promised to accomplish a very important goal for Him while here on earth. Both Khaos and Kunfuzion wanted to make sure they passed this notion on to their kittens.

He remembered Khaos saying, "All our experiences in life happen to remind us of the talents we were given to accomplish our main purpose for being here. Fulfilling our contract really isn't an option." Kunfuzion felt this was pretty powerful. They would wait for the right time to divulge this secret. It was a big part of getting smart, but that took time, and the timing had to be just right.

Even when she was young, Khaos had always known she had a special talent helping other cats see important things that could make their lives better. That was her special gift and her main purpose in life. On the other hand, Kunfuzion took awhile to fully understand his main talent and purpose.

Eventually he realized that he was exceptionally gifted at understanding how other cats learned. He was especially talented in helping cats with learning disabilities learn as much as they could. He was even successful in helping many cats graduate from college when they didn't originally have the confidence or skills to do that. Khaos pointed out this talent to him. Even though Kunfuzion already sensed it, this added much satisfaction to what he was doing.

Naturally they both thought this talent thing was true for all the other cats; each had a special talent he or she needed to develop and use to better the cat world. This seemed to be a reasonable assumption.

Khaos had her platform, "Some cats' special talent could be instructing others how to catch mice better. For others it could be showing some cats how to get their human owners to let them out for a run. Still for others, it could be teaching all the kittens how to meow better for their supper. Finding and using the special gift you have is the best way to be thankful for the nine lives you were given." This made purrfect sense.

Khaos and Kunfuzion planned to encourage their kittens to try several things to make sure they could uncover their special talents. Because they were exceptionally bright and multi-talented, they knew their kittens would be too. But they also knew that sometimes cats would start doing what they did best without even knowing it. They might even feel that what they were doing wasn't really good enough to be their main purpose in life.

They decided that discovering your special talent was just a matter of looking to see what activities you enjoyed most. As usual, there was no need to make this more difficult or complicated than it needed to be. The two partners were on a roll, and so they kept going on to their last do suggestion, before earning a much-deserved nap, this time in the guest bedroom.

By now, Khaos and Kunfuzion were getting excited about the prospects of parenthood and about the opportunity to apply their own special talents as parents. After all, that hard work with the mouse conspiracy had to pay off sooner or later.

Do Suggestion #10: Improve and Grow.

> *Life is a precious gift. Don't waste it on being unhappy, dissatisfied, or anything less than you can be.*
>
> —Kunfuzion's grandmother

Khaos and Kunfuzion decided to save this suggestion for last since they knew it was one of the more important things they had both learned about life. They also wanted to take their time offering a good explanation, because it was kind of tricky.

They had discovered that the main purpose of their lives was to grow and improve in everything they were doing, from sleeping, to eating, to playing, to applying their special talents to making the cat world a better place for all the other cats. Of course, they didn't like being forced to improve or told they had to change. Rather they preferred to do it on their own, naturally, at their own speed, much like their kittens would probably prefer.

Even though they thought this self-improvement and growth process was probably the same for all cats and everything else in the whole wide universe, they also realized each cat had to uncover this profound truth all by him or herself. This was something somebody else couldn't tell you.

So the task was to figure out how to guide their kittens to see what they themselves were seeing so clearly, without being imposing. They knew everyone had to do it his or her own way, but they certainly didn't want to watch their own kittens fall down too many times or waste too many of their nine lives. This would require them to use their smartness and their special talents.

Khaos and Kunfuzion now knew this was going to have to be a two-part plan. First they would give unconditional love to their kittens and be certain they felt totally loved and accepted the way they were or wanted to be.

This was going to be difficult, especially if one of their kittens wanted to be an alley cat or, heavens forbid, a tree climber. Or worse yet, one might want to marry a longhaired, mixed breed Tabby who had no culture or education.

But what will be, will be, and to be successful in changing another cat for the better, you have to accept and understand him or her right now, without any changes. This expectation of how others need to change is what ruins most cat relationships.

Once a cat feels secure, he or she is free to grow and make improvements naturally. This is a normal part of life that most cats resist for as long as they can. But sooner or later they realize that growing, making improvements, and getting better is more natural than resisting change.

The second part of the plan was to demonstrate their own willingness to grow and improve along with their kittens. Over the years, they had learned the importance of being a good role model. Most cats learn from what they see, not what they hear. Cats are seers and smellers, not hearers.

One thing Khaos and Kunfuzion pledged to do was to keep up their own appearances. Like it or not, a cat's appearance is often the most important thing in being successful. Not all cats are lucky enough to be handsome and beautiful, but they can certainly show themselves in the best light by smiling a lot, wearing stylish collars, keeping trim, flossing, and grooming themselves regularly, especially getting their ears cleaned and the sleep gook out of their eyes. Eyes are very important. So are smiles.

Khaos and Kunfuzion just had to resist the temptation to speed this whole growth and improvement process up. They didn't have to! They would all grow and improve together naturally as a family. They would resist their tendency to rush things. Now they were ready for a good nap, followed by some fabulously delicious gourmet seafood or maybe some turkey and gravy. If they meowed just right they might even get some of Toot's leftover chocolate mousse for desert.

The Don't List

If you don't get everything you want, think of all the things you don't get that you don't want.
—Oscar Wilde

After a few hours of peaceful resting, the two cats woke up. Not being inclined to be negative, both Khaos and Kunfuzion hesitated a little in making any negative "don't" suggestions right off the bat. However, they realized some negative expression is a normal part of life and to exclude it would be painting too rosy of a picture for their kittens. They decided to keep this list simple with one or two practical reasons for not doing these things and maybe a positive way to turn the don't into a do.

Don't Suggestion #1: Don't Hurry.

A youth becomes an adult when the marks he wants to leave on the world have nothing to do with tires.
—unknown drag racer

This was one of the more important lessons Kunfuzion had learned by overcoming his own hyperactivity. After years of going 1,000 mph and never finishing anything or even getting much of anything done, he started slowing down to keep things in better focus. This wasn't easy because at first he had to get rid of his tendency to hurry up. When he was finally able to stop, what he saw was amazing: There is much more time than you can ever possibly imagine. His trick was to start living every moment as if it were his last, and then suddenly every moment began to last much longer.

Khaos offered some practical reasons to not hurry or rush: "First, when you rush, you usually do a lousy job and then just have to start all over again. That is a waste of good time and usually costs you something. Second, when you hurry, you are missing part of the enjoyment you could get in doing something slower."

"And finally," she continued, "when you try to hurry up and get smart too quickly, you may miss learning the things that will help you get smart. For instance, instead of being too quick to give answers maybe you should think of a better question to ask."

Khaos wasn't always aware of the positive effect she had on Kunfuzion. Her new practicality often stimulated him into seeing other worthwhile things. He added, "Yes, I agree it is good to slow down and not rush around or hurry too much, but maybe there are a few things you do want to speed up."

"Like what?" asked Khaos.

Kunfuzion explained, "Like hurrying up to do things you don't like to do so you have more time to do the things you enjoy."

"That makes good sense," agreed Khaos, realizing it might be the right time to stop what they were doing and do something else. The trouble is she enjoyed working on this project and she enjoyed playing too. On that note they were both ready for some nonsensical play and then maybe a nap.

Don't Suggestion #2: Don't Quit.

> *Success is going from failure to failure without losing enthusiasm.*
> —Winston Churchill

Khaos was the one whose father taught her this value. However, her father just created situations for her to practice sticking things out. Quitting wasn't an option when growing up in the cat world out in the country. It was a sign of weakness, and nobody thought much of you if you were a quitter.

Obviously times had changed, and both Khaos and Kunfuzion felt this was an important value to teach their kittens. Khaos was always thankful her father hadn't allowed her to quit things too easily. Later when things really got tough, she was strong enough to hang in there and not quit like some of the other cats.

"So how do we explain the importance of not quitting?" asked Kunfuzion. Khaos responded, "Let's start by saying that quitting is such an easy habit to pick up, but one that you can't stop very easily. The more you quit, the easier it becomes and the harder it is to stop. In that light, it is a dangerous habit that can get the best of you before you know it. It just isn't very smart to let a negative habit control you so much."

Kunfuzion liked that direct explanation, even though it bordered on being slightly unclear. He did have something else to add. "But you need to know that there are a few times when quitting is smart," he reminded his partner. "Remember that you need to learn how to quit bad habits while you still can. And also, you have to know when you are beaten." Both cats knew about Doc's many matrimonial failures that went on too long because he didn't know how to do either.

Both cats also thought about all the humans in Las Vegas and Atlantic City who didn't know when they had lost enough money. Their pet cats were doomed to cheap brand dry cat food—when they were lucky enough to get it. And they were certainly not going to get any stylish collars, designer food bowls, or grooming sessions at PetsMart.

The direction of this discussion was starting to make Khaos feel a little guilty thinking about her weekly three-dollar expenditures for cat

Powerball tickets at the local Motomart (Doc picked them up for her). So she started talking about food, as it was chow time for them both!

Don't Suggestion #3: Don't Lie.

If you tell the truth you don't have to remember anything.
—Mark Twain

I will handle this one all by myself," volunteered Kunfuzion. "Just like Mark Twain said, 'It is much easier to tell the truth because you don't ever have to remember anything,'" he uttered in one breath. In another one he added, "Besides, when you start lying, somebody else will always be smart enough to catch you in the act and then what do you do?"

Khaos couldn't just sit there and let Kunfuzion do all the talking. She had learned a few things about lying too. She spoke slowly, "One of the worst things you can do is to lie about lying. When somebody catches you in a lie, it is time to fess up. Lying about lying becomes unforgivable. Remember the last few presidents in the human world?" "Yes," said Kunfuzion. "I remember one who even creatively redefined what lying was so that he couldn't be considered a liar legally."

"If you lie and get caught and admit it, you are usually forgiven, but if you keep on lying, nobody will ever trust you again. I don't know about you, but I want to be trusted." Kunfuzion was quite satisfied with his own simple explanation of not having to remember anything when you told the truth. He didn't have a very good memory. Besides, being deceitful bothered his conscience.

Both cats saw a need to go a step further with this idea of always telling the truth, knowing that the cultural norm was quickly changing. Even the definition of "truth" was taking on new meanings.

They silently agreed to always be consistent in defining lying for their kittens: lying was not telling the truth, and truth is simply what is or isn't so. Neither cat had a hard time seeing the difference between telling a lie and telling the truth because they had always been taught that anything short of the truth was a lie. Why did it need to be more complicated?

Khaos and Kunfuzion promised themselves they would both strive very hard to avoid telling even little harmless fibs, because they knew that was where lying started. Having their kittens be totally honest in dealing with their friends would be a high priority. They would encourage total honesty around the house by not asking accusatory questions that usually begged for lies.

Don't Suggestion #4: Don't Be Dishonest.

> *Life is like a bank. You have to make deposits before you can make withdrawals. Dishonesty is trying to make a withdrawal before you make a deposit and results in a debt with high interest.*
>
> —Toots

How do we teach our kittens to be honest?" asked Kunfuzion, knowing that things were going from black and white to gray and grayer these days. "Like any of these other suggestions," responded Khaos, "we have to be consistent in showing our own honesty to the kittens and then casually work in some practical benefits to being honest themselves."

"Sounds like a good plan," said Kunfuzion, "but we need to be prepared to explain how dishonesty seems to be rewarded sometimes.

Khaos and Kunfuzion remembered how they had learned the lesson of being honest. It started by seeing the effects of the wise cats saying "What goes around comes around." When they were dishonest with other cats, more dishonesty just came back to them in bigger and worse forms. When they were honest, they received honesty in return. This was the simple law of karma that usually took most cats a lifetime to learn.

At one point in this project, Khaos was flirting with the possibility of telling their future kittens that this Karma notion was the only thing that they would ever have to master in order to be happy, successful, and content. But she thought that would be too simple, too direct, and too obvious. Such qualities warn cats that things might be a little too easy. After all, there is no such thing as a free cat lunch. Khaos dismissed this temptation and got back to the more concrete consequences of dishonesty she and Kunfuzion had experienced living in their new home.

When Kunfuzion ate some of Khaos' food, Toots would move him to the laundry room where he had to smell the litter box when he was starving out of his little cat mind. When Khaos would hide and not come out of the bedroom when Doc called her, Doc would shake the irresistible treat can, not give her any treats, and then close the bedroom door for a few days. When the two cats started becoming more honest with Doc, Toots, and other neighborhood cats, Doc, Toots, and the other cats started being more honest with them.

Both honesty and dishonesty are highly contagious, they both recalled. It was Khaos who finally saw what was happening and said, "When you are being dishonest with others, you are really just cheating yourself—and you will never let yourself get away with it. You will be the one who will eventually catch your own hand in the cookie jar."

Kunfuzion knew that was one of those Khaos statements that needed to be repeated until the real meaning finally sunk in. At first he believed what Khaos was saying, in his own cat head, but now he understood what the words meant in his cat bones. That was part of the process of getting smart. Your head had to believe it, your heart had to support it, and your hands had to do it. Then you knew it in your bones. The head, heart, and hands team had real power.

Khaos realized she had forgotten to start out this suggestion with her usual technique; in case her ideas about honesty and dishonesty were not the same as her kittens, she immediately rectified the situation. "Honesty," she said, "is being truthful, and being truthful is only doing that which can't do any harm. Obviously, dishonesty is doing anything that can cause harm."

Then Khaos remembered something helpful that Kunfuzion had told her one day when they were talking about trust and dishonesty. Kunfuzion had said, "When you finally learn to let go and completely trust that life will give you your share of things, then your dishonest intentions and dishonest acts no longer serve a purpose." That was so heavy, both cats began to get sleepy. Obviously, it was time for another nap.

Don't Suggestion #5: Don't Gossip.

> *If all men knew what others say of them, there would not be four friends in the world.*
>
> —Blaise Pascal

In the cat world the female cats were the worst gossipers, so Kunfuzion decided to take a back seat to this one and let Khaos do all the talking. He might add something at the end if Khaos forgot something really important, but that wasn't likely.

Actually they both took a strong stance against gossiping. They had seen many other kittens worrying and crying over needless, mean-spirited gossip that was told about them. What always started out as an innocent conversation had a strange way of ending up hurting some poor kittens who weren't even able to defend themselves. There just wasn't any good purpose in this sort of behavior, and it really wasn't so innocent either. Gossiping was just another way of being dishonest and lying. And it certainly caused harm, which sometimes couldn't be undone.

Khaos was into self-improvement and realized long ago that gossip is a dishonorable, worthless activity that can only hurt others unfairly. Her main advice was, "If you have to gossip, spread positive gossip about others."

She knew that normal gossip hurt cats' reputations because the information one cat would tell another was usually half-wrong and always uncomplimentary. Plus, you never knew how much gossip flavored other cats' perceptions of you. Rarely did you ever have a chance to correct these wrong perceptions made from malicious gossip. Often, what you didn't know hurt you.

The guiding rule Khaos wanted her kittens to follow was: "If you want to tell one cat something about another cat, always ask yourself, for what purpose do I want to tell this information? If it is not for the right reason and it might be harmful, don't say it." Kunfuzion then tried to remind his sister of something he had overheard Toots say to Doc. He paraphrased, "Sometimes gossip is the way kittens learn valuable social skills about what they say and then what happens." Khaos wasn't often domineering in his views, but this is one time she dismissed Toots' advice as being too risky. It was just something to stay away from altogether. Kunfuzion wasn't really in the mood to pursue the issue any further, so he let it go.

Khaos thought that most gossip was just a misguided way to gain acceptance by another cat. Some cats felt important gossiping and telling "secrets" to other cats. She knew there were more positive ways to be accepted and feel important. One way was to ask another cat questions about himself or herself and take interest in the answers. Another way was to do something good that helped another cat and then not brag about it or expect anything in return. These kinds of positive behaviors always got better results.

There was nothing more Kunfuzion could add to this discussion about gossiping, so he suggested they take a short play break. Naturally Khaos was in agreement. It was nice when they both agreed so easily. They were even beginning to master the art of agreeing to disagree, which was a very valuable skill in the cat world.

Don't Suggestion #6: Don't Be Irresponsible.

You can't escape the responsibility of tomorrow by evading it today.
—Abraham Lincoln

Kunfuzion had recently taught a cat seminar on responsibility, so this topic was still fresh on his mind. His main advice for their kittens was to realize that there are always positive or negative consequences for each of the many choices they would make in life. He wanted their kittens to notice the connection between the choices they make and the results they get. This is the best possible check on knowing what to do.

The object of good choosing is to always make the choices that have the best consequences. You need to slow down and think about what you are doing to understand your response-ability each and every time. For instance, if someone says something unkind, you have many options. You can get hurt and mad or say something unkind in return. You can also walk away and ignore the person altogether. Or, you can let the other person know how their words made you feel.

There is always an option to be aggressive, passive, or assertive. Being assertive always seems to work best, because it involves doing something that is positive and not harmful to yourself or others. It is the only win-win choice, and it doesn't take a rocket scientist to see that. Assertiveness always gets good results.

"No one could argue with this," said Khaos, "but why do so many cats make so many bad choices?" What she was meaning to say was, "Why did I make so many bad choices?"

"That is an excellent question," responded Kunfuzion to the real question. "Once you goof up and make a bad choice, then you may be forced to make another choice you may not particularly want to make in order to get back to the place where the better choices are. And when you make the wrong choice and exude negativity, you always get more negativity back and then you want to get back at that—and by then you have forgotten who started it."

Kunfuzion continued, "It is too easy to get lazy and weak and give up once things start going downhill. That is when you have to accept responsibility for getting yourself to the place where you really don't want to be and working extra hard to get out." At that point he remembered something funny he had heard, which was, "When you are in a hole, quit digging."

"Sometimes," concluded Kunfuzion, "so many wrong choices get made that it all seems hopeless. Although you can't make one big choice to wipe away all the past, you can make a small choice to start all over again right now." He recalled an impressive quote in one of Doc's psychology books. It was something to the effect of "Every long journey begins with one small step."

The dialogue was getting a bit abstract, so Khaos, pressed for a concrete example. "Okay, Kunfuzion explained, "Do you remember Doc's problems when he didn't have a job?" "Yes," answered Khaos, "those were some tough times for both he and Toots."

"First he had to accept part of the blame for making some really bad choices that helped him lose his job, like leaving his family and not fully appreciating his job when he had it. Then he had to start all over again and even consider taking a job that didn't pay very well or use his skills, just to be able to pay some bills. He even had to consider moving somewhere he didn't like. This all helped him clarify what was really most important in his life so he could start making the right choices again

"You know the rest of the story. Fortunately, he accepted responsibility and started making better choices. It wasn't easy, but in a way he didn't have any other choice, so to speak. One right choice led to a better one, just like one bad choice led to a worse one earlier."

Don't Suggestion #7: Don't Judge.

> *Good judgment comes from experience. Experience comes from bad judgment.*
>
> —Evan Hardin

Kunfuzion was non-judgmental by nature and taught Khaos much about the value of this approach. He had explained earlier that if we are all judging each other critically, then nobody gets anywhere. Besides, nobody listens to criticism for which he or she didn't ask. It is too easy to be critical and judgmental about other cat's deficiencies, and we all have our own. When we are talking about other cats' hairballs, bad breath, plumpness, and limp hair, we are usually just talking about ourselves.

Kunfuzion had learned a lesson from one of his teachers that stuck with him: "If you are going to spend time criticizing another cat about how he or she is doing something, then spend some more time showing that cat how to do it better." This made very good sense to Khaos. Kunfuzion felt good when he thought back upon all the times that he had applied this important advice. The only thing he regretted was not thanking his teacher. He secretly hoped the teacher might read this book.

"How do we teach our kittens not to judge others when that is probably all they will see their classmates do in school," asked a puzzled Khaos. "I guess all we can do is remind them that being judged always results in bad feelings and keeps cats from getting along," replied Kunfuzion. I suppose another way is to not be guilty of judging our kittens ourselves," added Khaos.

"When they do something silly or something we don't approve of, we don't have to make them feel like idiots or bad, mentally deficient kittens."

Then Kunfuzion thought of a practical lesson. They would encourage their kittens to work on little creative projects like making paper birdhouses or playing mousetraps, and then they wouldn't judge the results. They both thought back to their own school experiences and realized why it took them both so long to develop their creative talents.

It seemed, everyone, everywhere was judging too much. Judgment destroys creativity, and cats need as much creativity as they can get to solve all the cat problems in the cat world today. Moreover, creativity is a fundamental need of a cat's soul. Today's inclination for spiritual development uncovered that fact. The two cats mutually agreed that *judgment* would be a word they would strike from their vocabulary. In a broader sense, they would save their judgment about life until life was over.

Don't Suggestion #8: Don't Worry.

> *Worrying or complaining about problems is like trying to sweep dirt with a broom that has no bristles or eat soup with a fork.*
>
> —Kunfuzion

Khaos was not much of a worrier, even though maybe she should have been at times. Admittedly, she was too carefree. Kunfuzion worried too much, but mostly about the future. Together they kept a good balance.

They agreed to help each other. Kunfuzion would teach Khaos to plan for the future while Khaos would show Kunfuzion how to live more in the now. Their solution was simple but powerful. They agreed to take action to fix whatever might be a cause for worry so that they wouldn't have anything to worry about. In the process of helping each other, they realized that the negative energy of worrying could be replaced by the positive energy of preventative action. Then with all the energy they had wasted on worrying about worrying, they could play more. Compounding negativity was a real waste of time and energy. Thank heavens they had figured that out. Negativity is an addiction to be avoided.

This was a great plan. It was one of those rare, simple solutions to a problem that actually worked. They became so good at it that they decided a long, complicated, written suggestion against worrying wasn't necessary. They wouldn't demonstrate any needless worrying for their kittens to see. That way they wouldn't be teaching a bad habit to be avoided.

"One last detail," said Khaos wanting to work it in at the last moment. "This has to do with complaining. Complaining is just an extension of worrying. When you complain, you just want someone else to assume responsibility for a situation or thing you don't like."

"Good point," complimented Kunfuzion. "We will teach our kittens to be assertive and take responsibility for doing something about a situation they don't like instead of wasting their time complaining about it. And we will not complain ourselves. Just positive action."

This was enough on this topic because any more explanation would be overkill. They were both highly educated cats, having gone to the finest cat schools available, but they had learned the importance of clarity and simplicity. Besides, it was nap time again, and so off they went to the basement because it was cooler down there. It was getting too hot upstairs these days, and they needed some very good rest to finish their list of suggestions properly. The best was to come.

Don't Suggestion #9 Don't Wander.

Keep your face to the sunshine
and you cannot see the shadow.
—Helen Keller

After a long refreshing nap, Khaos was extremely clear-headed and anxious to get their project completed. She had never quite learned how to control her tendency to want to hurry up and finish things. Kunfuzion was hoping this was something she would learn to improve on before the kittens came. Maybe he would just have to help Khaos do this.

"You'll have to excuse me, Kunfuzion. I am going to get a little deep on you with this one," started Khaos. Kunfuzion prepared himself since he was already beginning to wonder what this wandering thing was all about. Sometimes his partner got into some bad tuna fish that adversely affected her thinking capacity. However, Khaos had smartly anticipated the possible objection, so she went back to her old technique of defining a thing before any misunderstanding got started.

"By not wandering," began Khaos, "I mean not forgetting your roots—who you really are and where you started from. In a much deeper sense, I also mean not losing touch with your main purpose in life—to develop your talents and learn to use them to make life better for as many cats as you can. Another way to say this is to not forget the Golden Rule we spoke of earlier." Khaos sensed she might already be getting too deep so she stopped there.

Kunfuzion, however, began to see all sorts of possibilities with this suggestion. His main insight was to realize the importance of keeping a balanced position in everything. That way he was able to gain a much better view in all directions. Then he would remind himself not to wander too far away from that point, which was always the best seat in the house. Plus, from there, he could always see home.

He said, "I hope we can teach our kittens the value of being assertive in both taking care of themselves and respecting others, to try and satisfy both their wants and their needs, to think and feel, work and play, and to enjoy life and be good too."

Both cats knew that once you got too far out of balance you start feeling poorly, and that getting back in balance from there is very hard work. By then you are out of practice. You can even get so far out of practice from making too many wrong choices that you forget where the road back home is. Then you are lost.

Khaos, in particular, realized the importance of moderation and keeping herself in balance, but she had learned that lesson the hard way. She wished someone had impressed her enough to listen to this lesson instead of wandering all over the universe in her own journey, some of which wasn't exactly fun or enjoyable. She admitted to herself awhile back that she had taken the long way around to get back home.

Kunfuzion asked, "Do you really think you would have listened?" "Probably not," was her honest answer. "I had to do it my way," she thought silently. Kunfuzion knew that was also true for himself. The two cats had learned to communicate with complete openness and honesty, just like Doc and Toots.

So, they were both about to arrive at a critical, but inevitable conclusion. Kunfuzion was first to speak, "Can we really teach our kittens all these valuable suggestions, or will they just have to learn their own lessons the hard way like we did?"

Khaos thought for a moment and then said, "I think we should follow our own suggestions here and do all these things ourselves as parents. We can look for opportunities to apply particular suggestions when our kittens present us with a real-life problem or situation. And sometimes we can create situations to teach some of these lessons. More than anything, we should remain open to the possibility that our kittens will give us some entirely new suggestions. We will probably learn as much being parents as we will teach our kittens."

Getting very observant, Kunfuzion said, "Isn't this what our parents tried to do?" "Yes," answered Khaos, "We're back home again after a bit of our own wandering."

At least the two prospective parents had taken the time to carefully think out a reasonable game plan for their parenting before they just fumbled around in the dark. Sometimes how you are trying to do something isn't as important as what you are doing. Even if the parenting plan was mostly for their own peace of mind in getting the important things sorted out, all their efforts were worth it.

Now the two cats could go practice the special technique of nap-taking which they had perfected during this exercise. They would dream of being good parents and using their special talents to apply all the practical suggestions they had just planned.

This would probably be an especially long nap since there was so much to dream about. They would need the rest too. The cat world was moving so fast that by the time they woke up, values might have changed so drastically that they would have to rewrite some of these suggestions. Being smart cats though, they felt confident they had selected the core values that weren't likely to change. This is part of the wisdom they had learned.

Just to be on the safe side, they were already prepared by having previously learned the importance of flexibility, open-mindedness, and adaptability to change. And as their ace in the hole, they both trusted life completely now and knew in their cat souls that they would be able to handle anything that came their way. They knew the way of life, and they had the genuine spiritual power to teach their kittens how to have a head, heart, and hands team. As they slept they both had peaceful smiles on their faces. They could see their kittens being happy, successful, and content.

During their unusually long nap that night something very peculiar happened. Both Khaos and Kunfuzion had exactly the same dream. They both dreamed that Doc and Toots had left them a note on the computer screen. The note read:

Dear Khaos and Kunfuzion,

You have done well with this parenting plan. Congratulations! We just have one minor suggestion. Try to understand this basic reality: When you finally start becoming more aware of all the conscious and unconscious choices you are already making right now, then life will come to a complete halt where there is no time. This is a very special place. Listen very careful-

ly, and you will learn who you really are. Then everything will make sense.

Love, Doc & Toots

P.S. Good luck and try to figure out how to pass this last suggestion of ours on to your kittens. Or better yet, just figure it out for yourselves.

CHAPTER 10

Five Basic Questions

The quality of the answer has a lot to do with the quality of the question.
—deceased cat lawyer

A few months later, after finishing this project and fully digesting the brilliant note from Doc and Toots, Khaos and her brother Kunfuzion adopted two little kittens. Unlike the human practice of naming children at birth, cats prefer to wait and pick names that fit kittens' personalities more appropriately. So, they named their son Chaos and their daughter Clarity, for obvious reasons. All kittens have unique personalities and aren't as aloof and independent as most humans wrongly think.

Chaos enjoyed spreading confusion and complexity by creating gaps between where he and his sister were and where they wanted to be. Clarity, on the other hand, preferred the order, harmony, and simplicity of closing gaps and being where she and her brother wanted to be in the first place. Chaos was clever at creating confusing and complex chaos, but Clarity was just as adept at restoring simple and clear order. Together they had all bases covered.

Chaos slept during the day and played all night long. He played special tricks like digging tasty treats out of the trash can, cold-nosing Doc and Toots at four in the morning, sneaking into the shower for a drink, and hiding socks that he snatched from their dirty clothes hamper. He also did lots of other things Doc and Toots never knew about. Some things are better unknown. Of course, their parents, Khaos and Kunfuzion, knew everything that was going on, as smart Siamese cats usually do.

On the other side of the coin, Clarity tried to sleep peacefully in bed with Doc and Toots at night. During the daytime she ate, entertained herself with ordinary things like rocks, bugs, and paper, and watched birds play. When Toots and Doc came home from work, she would keep them entertained with her acrobatic antics and crawl up on their laps to watch TV, while her brother went off for some sleep in preparation for a long night of mischief. On occasions he would sneak out and try to bite Toots' toes when she was all cuddled up napping with Clarity on the couch. This was unwanted and unwelcome behavior.

Needless to say, these differences were a challenge for Khaos and Kunfuzion, not to mention Doc and Toots. The lessons they had learned from their mousetrap conspiracy and the experience they gained from developing their parenting plan were surely tested. At this point, the new cat parents began to think they needed a more effective approach to guide their kittens. Like all good plans this one needed some rethinking and maybe even some major modifications. Things always sound good on paper, but reality has a funny way of changing everything.

The two new parents consulted their own adoptive "parents" about this problem. During the past year they had all learned to communicate quite well. Doc gave them a useful strategy. He suggested they post a list of five basic questions everyone, including cats, has about work and life in general. These important questions would stimulate the two kittens to think and ask questions of their own. Then Khaos and Kunfuzion could work in all the advice they had put together in their parenting plan and even add new insights they might learn along the way.

So, Khaos and Kunfuzion went off to the local Cat Office Max to get the supplies they needed for this new project. They got some great new magic markers and colored poster board. Kunfuzion was the artist in the family so he began to neatly print the questions for the notice they would place near the food bowls. After an hour or so, they had the sign ready to go. It read:

Five Basic Questions All Cats Need to Answer:

- What is it I am supposed to be doing here?
- How am I supposed to be doing it?
- How do I know if I am doing it right?
- What's in it for me?
- Where can I go when I need help?

Khaos was the cautious one, and she suggested they discuss possible answers they could give to Chaos and Clarity when they asked these five questions. They mutually decided to set up a five-day schedule to do the preparation work. Then they would hang the poster over the weekend. Here's how the next week went.

Monday: What is it I am supposed to be doing here?

Both cats agreed this was probably the most important question any kitten could ever have. But they both realized some cats didn't even know the answer to this question. They scratched their heads and finally decided that the main answer they would give their kittens would be a two-parter. At first they would be blunt with their conviction that all cats had to discover the unique purpose they were supposed to carry out in exchange for the opportunity to live as a cat. This was each cat's main contribution he would carry out with the help of his special talents.

They knew from their own experience that finding the answer to this question is extremely difficult. The best answers to all the really important questions are often so simple and obvious that they go unnoticed. Most often, a cat has to look back and discover where all his life experiences have taken him before he can recognize exactly where he is at the present. A cat needs to take the time to look back in order to see his purpose more clearly. Then he can see what he does best and enjoys most.

In the meantime, while Chaos and Clarity tried to discover their main purpose, the two parents would encourage the kittens to concentrate on being the best at whatever they were doing at the time, whether it be sleeping, eating, playing with other kittens, chasing mice, watching birds, learning at kitten school, working at their chosen job, or being a parent themselves.

Khaos and Kunfuzion were pleased with their planned approach to this first important question. Besides, they had already found good answers to this question in their earlier parenting plan. They were ready for Tuesday's discussion, but for right now, an afternoon nap seemed appealing. A good mixture of work and play would be good role-modeling behavior to demonstrate for their two kittens. They were committed to being teaching parents.

Tuesday: How am I supposed to do it?

Kunfuzion was the first to speak about this question. He said, "You know Khaos, maybe this is the one question we can't really answer. This is where we are all free to come up with our own unique answer. You remember saying you had to do it your own way, don't you?"

Khaos quickly replied, "Yes, and so did Frank Sinatra and Elvis Presley," trying to work in a little humor.

"But on a serious note," she continued, "We don't want to spend too much time concentrating on how to do something and not enough time on what we should be doing, which only brings us back to the importance of the first question.

"In the consulting work Doc does, he encourages leaders and managers to determine what their employees are supposed to do, but to allow the employees to figure out how they want to do it. That way both groups give input and there is real teamwork." Kunfuzion wondered in his little cat mind whether this was the same for life in general.

As a result of this discussion, both cats promised that they wouldn't even try to answer this question for their kittens. This would be something Chaos and Clarity would have to figure out themselves. The two new parents were quickly learning important lessons from all the valuable work they had already done in developing their parenting plan. They were having fun and enjoying their success too. As Doc observed Khaos and Kunfuzion discuss these things, he realized he was learning a lot too.

Wednesday: How will I know if I am doing it right?

Khaos suggested, "We might begin the answer to this question by reminding our kittens of their good minds, intuitions, and consciences. When you think about something hard enough and follow your intuitive feelings and guidance from your conscience, it always turns out for the best."

Kunfuzion agreed but put it a little differently, "When you are doing the right thing you get the consequences and the results you want. And if by chance you don't like the consequences and results you get, try doing something different until you get everything right."

"That's quite a mouthful," thought Khaos silently, but she couldn't find a flaw in her brother's reasoning. When Khaos noticed the connection between the choices she made and the consequences she got, she managed to take more control of herself. She also stopped making so many bad choices.

Both Khaos and Kunfuzion realized that their discussion took them right back to the wisdom of the Golden Rule: Do onto others, as you would have them do onto you. By now they realized that everyone tends to make things more complicated than they need to be, perhaps out of boredom or just to make things more challenging. They now had a chaos-creating gap-spreader for a son and an order-restoring gap-closer for a daughter. Things would never get boring for them! What a challenge to try and get them to see the same thing the same way.

Thursday: What's in it for me?

Khaos and Kunfuzion were beginning to think this was getting easy but soon the difficulty of helping their kittens arrive at the best answer to this question confronted them. Kunfuzion started this discussion by saying, "We always want to know what rewards we are going to get when we play by Doc and Toots' rules. How will it be different with our rules and our kittens?" "It won't be," said Khaos. Then there was a long silence while the two parents began thinking back to see the answer they had each come up with to resolve this particular dilemma.

"First of all," remembered Khaos, "You only get the right results by doing the right things. The right results not only give you a real sense of satisfaction and accomplishment, but they also lead to success. What could possibly be fairer than that chain of events?"

Again, Kunfuzion put it a little differently, "When you finally learn to give more you get more. Then, when you finally figure out what you are supposed to be doing with your life and start doing it, you end up getting everything you ever wanted and then some."

"Well said," concluded Khaos, realizing she couldn't top that answer. This was getting easier, but they had struggled several cat years to discover these answers. They were beginning to see they probably wouldn't have much luck at making things easier for their kittens. Their own parents loved them and tried hard, but... This wasn't cat pessimism, just cat reality.

Kunfuzion summarized something important that he had learned. He said, "I first began to feel more happy and content when I learned how to appreciate and enjoy all the ordinary things that I already had right in front of me."

Khaos added her two cents, "For me the turning point was in realizing the pastures on the other side of the fence aren't always greener." Doc overheard this last comment and enjoyed a good chuckle, having had the same insight himself earlier. But he did think it was odd that cats and humans could have the same experiences.

Friday: Where can I go when I need help?

At daybreak on Friday, it suddenly dawned upon Khaos and Kunfuzion that getting their kittens to evewn ask this question would probably be their main parenting contribution. They decided to make another poster to hang near the litter box. It would read: "Don't drown in a swimming pool by allowing your foolish pride to keep you from yelling 'help' for a lifeguard to save you!"

Khaos and Kunfuzion made a pledge that they would ask for Chaos and Clarity's help whenever they needed it. In return they would work on being approachable and available when the kittens needed their help. Most of all, they would not impose their answers to the other four questions until Chaos and Clarity asked them. They knew that giving help when it wasn't requested just resulted in unnecessary frustration and resentment.

With this wise insight, they knew their parenting plan was getting close to the point of perfection, and that any more planning might be wasted effort. They were ready to practice all these do's and don'ts and answer these five questions by demonstrating the answers with their everyday behavior. By now they had realized this wasn't as much a parenting plan for their kittens as it was a self-development plan for themselves. Now that was a plan!

All their efforts deserved some fresh surf and turf and maybe even a lick of red Shiraz from down-under. After that, it would be time for a very long nap. They had worked hard and deserved to eat and rest. Plus, now they knew all the real work would soon begin, and they would need plenty of energy.

But Kunfuzion had saved the best for last. He reminded his brother that everything in the whole universe could ask God for help when it was needed, and He was the best person to ask. Both cats agreed that they would teach their kittens the fine art of praying for help correctly. "Most cats" she said, "make the mistake of asking for more mice, toys, food, birds, and nap time. And they often ask for a problem to go away all by itself. What they really want is the wisdom, strength, and courage to see how they are responsible for contributing to the problem and then to make it go away through their own efforts." Kunfuzion meowed approval.

Doc and Toots smiled proudly, watching the four cats enjoy their gourmet meal (a few drops of wine included) and then take a peaceful family catnap. They silently congratulated themselves for first being good "parents" and now good "grandparents." Their own parents and grandparents were probably smiling somewhere too. Things were good at this quiet house on the lake. Now they all knew how to have their cheese and eat it too.

Conclusion to Part II

If you live in the present, every moment is a new beginning.
—Khaos' real grandfather

There have been many useful ideas presented by cats and mice in the attempt to spell out a prescription for how to have your cheese and eat it too. Here is a summary of the most important ideas of this prescription:

• No matter what you may be doing, you are trying to fit in and make what you are fitting into better. Most of us start out in a frenzy to change things to our liking before we even know what we need to fit into. This is why we think we can't have our cheese and eat it too. Learn to fit in first. Then change things from the inside out. Start with yourself.

• Recognize and accept the part you play in creating confusion so you can have something to do when sorting through it. Then realize just because you see clearly and simply, you may not be through playing the game. Always try to know if you are creating confusion or restoring order, and do it the best you can.

• Take advantage of the power you have in teaching others by the way you are, not by what you say. Most importantly, your attitude in adversity outspeaks everything else.

• Stop automatically dividing life into *okay* and *not okay* sides. Look for creative ways to join things together such as thoughts and feelings, right and wrong, and this and that. Look for understanding rather than critical judgment.

• Pay attention to how you may be unlikable without knowing it. Strive to make improvements and become likable. It will help with everything else. Start with an incurably positive attitude, especially when things aren't going well.

• Understand miscommunication and never assume you understand or are understood without checking it out. Become a skilled talker, writer, listener, and reader.

• Confess to being responsible for even the craziest things you do while playing your own versions of the hide-and-seek games, and be very careful to avoid hiding where you won't ever get found.

• You have a brain, so use it fully. If quantity thinking causes problems, then quality thinking has to solve them. Start thinking about your own thinking. Think hard about some things and follow your intuition and conscience to make the right choices and get the results you want.

• Make an effort to become more sensitive to the importance of timing and to the little things you can do to have the biggest impact in closing the gap between where you are and where you want to be. Tune into the subtle connections and inter-relations between things.

• Discover the sacred contract you made in exchange for your life. Work to develop your special talents so you can be happy and successful at carrying out your unique purpose in life. Remember that you get to choose how to do this.

• Get important things done quickly so you can slow down enough to appreciate valuable things before they aren't around to be appreciated.

• If the grass in your pasture isn't green enough, fertilize and water it.

• Don't ever be timid about asking for help when you need it. Just learn to ask for the right things that will help the most.

• Give more than you take. The more you give, the more you get, guaranteed.

• Fit in better by avoiding the deadly mental mousetraps, practicing the do's and don'ts, answering the five critical questions, and understanding these other points. This is how you can have your cheese and eat it too. It is easier than you imagine.

While I still have your attention, let me conclude with one final idea. Maybe I am being presumptuous, but I don't really believe our cat and mouse leaders fully appreciated the amazing unity and strength of their Master Mousetrap Conspiracy Plan. The seven deadly psychological mousetraps all work together in a well-woven gestalt principle, meaning the whole is much stronger than the sum of its parts. In other words, all these individual mousetraps work together to form one very big mousetrap.

These seven psychological mousetraps are intricately inter-connected. For instance, babble can make you unlikable because you get too unbalanced from either-oring. Then instantaneousmania can impair any chance of quality thinking and dull sensitivity to problem-solving solutions you need to understand what is causing your unlikability. This, in turn, widens the gap between where you are and where you want to be. And then, of course, you may just be playing a hide-and-seek game to keep from being bored. Duncery, babble, and narcosis will keep this important realization from your awareness. What a mess this is to try and untangle! No small wonder there is so much chaos and confusion.

The clarification of all this chaos and confusion starts with answers to the five basic questions:

What am I supposed to be doing here?
How am I supposed to be doing it?
How do I know if I am doing it right?
What's in it for me?
Where can I go when I need help?

Practicing the do's and don'ts can help you get the best answers to these questions. *Having your cheese and eating it too is easier than you can ever imagine.* You really don't have to do much. All you have to do is let go, give in, and be natural. Then you will have all the cheese you could possibly want. You will also be happy, successful, and content.

Appendix A

Twenty Quick-and-Easy Ways to Have Your Cheese and Eat It Too

1. **Believe.** One of the most important sources of personal power is tied to the degree to which you believe you can influence reality enough to make your dreams come true. Although there are plenty of things that can happen in life to inhibit this belief and dampen your spirit, you still decide to believe or not to believe. Believing is the first step to being able to have your cheese and eat it too. Not believing will only take away cheese.

2. **Dream.** Start by dreaming about closing the bigger gap between where you are and where you want to be, but work mostly on closing the smaller gaps that make up this big one. A few of these smaller gaps are the ones between what you know and what you need to know, between what you say and what others hear,

between who you are and who you pretend to be, and between what you want and how clearly you can say it. The biggest little gap is the one between knowing all these things and actually doing something about them.

3. **Gain perspective.** Pay closer attention to the place from where you are looking and focus less on what you are seeing. Change viewpoints as often as you can, with the goal of getting closer to the middle where you can see in all directions. This is the best vantage point from which to make the right choices, especially those choices that will help you believe in your own personal power.

4. **Distinguish between wants and needs.** Let go of what your mind thinks it wants and give into what your soul knows it needs. Realize that you are just surrendering to yourself as part of your own plan. You are really just exchanging uncomfortable chaos and confusion for comfortable simplicity and clarity.

5. **Assess and adjust.** Slow down to get a clearer view of where you have been, where you are, and where you are going. Then make the necessary adjustments.

6. **Listen.** Listen more with both ears and talk less with one mouth so you can be surer of what you know and learn more at the same time.

7. **Ask questions.** Let your mouth ask questions to which your mind assumes the answers, and resist the temptation of asking questions to which you already know the answers.

8. **Be inclusive.** Dismiss only that which deeply offends your soul, and look for new and

unusual ways to include something about everything else.

9. **Value silence.** Learn the value of occasionally doing nothing or being strategically silent, especially in response to other people's problem behavior.

10. **Avoid bad habits.** Get to know what you are trying to avoid so that you can avoid it. Remember that all bad habits have payoffs, so find out what they are. In the meantime, focus on what you should be trying to do, such as being productive by eliminating wrong interpretations, controlling negative reactions, and planning positive actions.

11. **Look before entering.** Look for little doors that open bigger ones. If you are not sure, just take a quick peek before committing.

12. **Enjoy simple things.** Look at ordinary things with renewed amazement and curiosity and enjoy all the simple things of real wealth right under your nose before they disappear.

13. **Know what you want.** Learn to ask for the right things in the right way, but only after you have fully appreciated what you already have. Know what you want clearly enough to demand it when the time comes.

14. **Restore order.** Start putting things back together again that you took apart earlier and restore some order to the chaos you created. Begin by forgiving others and seeking forgiveness for such deeds.

15. **Seize the best, let go of the rest.** Free up some energy by concentrating on controlling the controllables and letting go of the rest. You

can do a much better job controlling the few things on the shorter list.

16. Replace quantity thinking with quality thinking. Especially replace oversized judgments with compact understanding. Increase more valuable brain space by forgetting unimportant things so you can remember the few important ones.

17. Practice responsible freedom. Pump up your passivity, tone down your aggression, and be appropriately assertive. Simply treat others the same way you want to be treated—with freedom and equality. Accept others, and at the same time challenge them to be better.

18. Stop the insanity. Stop expecting different results from doing the same thing the same way, over and over again. Vary your approach until you get the results you want, or vary what you want.

19. Be open. Be willing to let go, take risks, and make exchanges without expecting certain outcomes. Be more open to the possibilities without judgments.

20. Do the little things. Perfect the art of doing little things that get big results. A few of these "P" Points are being likable, maintaining a positive attitude during adversity, and remaining open-minded and tentative when you feel like being certain. Listen carefully, and be sensitive to the importance of timing in everything, especially knowing when you are nearing the point of no return. Finally, translate thought into action.

Appendix B

Twenty Cheese-Getting Action "P" Points

1. Ask your lover, best friend or mentor one small thing you could do to improve your likability. Listen closely and apply the answer, especially if you don't like it.

2. The next time a good thought pops into your mind, translate it immediately into action. If you fail to take the opportunity to do this, put the reason in writing.

3. Figure out how to pose intriguing questions to people in order to work in some useful knowledge you have that you are sure they need to know.

4. When you are asking anyone to do something for you, stop and think beforehand the precise expectations you have for the outcome and then plan out how to communicate those expectations effectively.

5. The next time you are inclined to tell someone else to "do more of this and less of that," invest some more time to figure out what you can take off the person's already over-loaded plate to make room for what you are trying to add.

6. Catch yourself in the next act of assuming and then verify your assumption by asking questions until you get an answer you can take to the bank. Always ask one more question than you think you need to ask.

7. Study a bad habit of yours in depth until you uncover the core problem and discover all the subtle, not-so-obvious payoffs that keep the behavior going.

8. Experiment with breaking out of a rut by being inconsistent in an insignificant way. You can even do something slightly wrong as long as it doesn't hurt anyone, including yourself.

9. When somebody is being obnoxious or intrusive, figure out a way to tell him or her in a subtle, witty and humorous way.

10. Practice having a positive attitude when you are feeling neutral. By doing this, your positive attitude will be available when you face hardship or adversity. Don't just think it, feel and show it.

11. Make a list of simple things of real wealth that are right under your nose and commit to enjoy those things everyday.

12. Take some time to evaluate your personal lifestyle and professional workplace in order to determine if you are actually living and practicing your most important values.

13. Find a powerful saying and display it where it will help you focus frequently on something that is important to you.

14. Practice making routine, insignificant decisions hastily and deliberate more than usual on the next difficult one that comes your way. Try using a grid to identify desirable and undesirable consequences, including costs, investments, and payoffs.

15. Raise the bar and do one bold thing in closing the gap between where you think you want to be and where you really want to be.

16. Look for ways to demonstrate a blending of opposing behaviors such as humility and confidence, leading and following, humor and seriousness, talking and listening, including and excluding, and simplicity and complexity.

17. At the end of the day make a list of a few critical things to follow-up and follow-through on the next day which will surely get some final results.

18. When you are headed for the next difficult discussion or conflict, take some time to plan productive communication by creating an easy-going, relaxed, non-defensive climate.

19. Find a way to improve your best skill or talent to become more of an expert at it.

20. Make a pledge to yourself to eliminate one major time waster to which you fall prey and carry it out. Use your new free time to work on other things

Appendix C

How Close Are You to Your Cheese?

Take the following test to see how close you are to having your cheese and eating it too. Circle the number that best represents your response to each of the following statements, according to the scale below. Then add up all the circled numbers for a grand total. Check your total score with the mileage chart at the end.

Scale:

5 = True as can be
3 = Getting better
1 = Needs work
0 = I am ashamed

1. I listen more than I talk, and I listen aggressively with both ears.

   5 3 1 0

2. I have big dreams, and I work hard to make them come true.

   5 3 1 0

3. I am in total control of my reactions.

   5 3 1 0

4. I do not make any assumptions without checking their validity.

   5 3 1 0

5. I live my life entirely around my most important values.

   5 3 1 0

6. I am always assertive.

   5 3 1 0

7. I am willing to let go, take risks, and make exchanges without expecting certain outcomes.

   5 3 1 0

8. I minimize worrying and complaining with preventative action.

   5 3 1 0

9. I have achieved balance in all areas of my life.

   5 3 1 0

10. I am able to slow down to see clearly where I have been and where I am now.

5 3 1 0

11. I know who I am, where I'm going, and how to get there.

5 3 1 0

12. I enjoy everything.

5 3 1 0

13. I find something to laugh about every day.

5 3 1 0

14. I never judge others before trying to understand them first.

5 3 1 0

15. I am completely honest.

5 3 1 0

16. I know how to ask for help when I need it.

5 3 1 0

17. I constantly work hard to improve and grow.

5 3 1 0

18. I use my intuition and creativity every day.

5 3 1 0

19. I always treat others as I want to be treated.

    5 3 1 0

20. I maintain a positive attitude even during adversity.

    5 3 1 0

21. I am involved in many worthwhile activities in my life.

    5 3 1 0

22. I never quit.

    5 3 1 0

23. I avoid gossiping at all times.

    5 3 1 0

24. I know what my talents are, have developed them fully, and use them frequently.

    5 3 1 0

25. I always make the right choices and get the best results.

    5 3 1 0

Total Score _______

Scoring:

0 to 30	=	You are continents away; shorten the distance to where you are going and pick up the speed. Focus.
31 to 65	=	You are still miles away; don't give up, keep trying.
66 to 99	=	You are getting closer! Run faster!
100 to 125	=	Congratulations! You have your cheese and are already eating it.

Suggested Reading

Light from any source is good.
—enlightened cat reader

Bennis, W. *Managing People Is Like Herding Cats*. Provo, UT: Executive Excellence Publishing, 1999.

Bentov, I. *Stalking the Wild Pendulum*. New York: E.P. Dutton, 1977.

Berne, E. *Games People Play*. New York: Grove Press, 1944.

Blanchard, K. *Leadership By The Book*. New York: William Morrow & Co., Inc., 1999.

Brown, H.J. *Live and Learn and Pass It On*. Los Angeles: Rutledge Press, 1991.

Bruner, J.S. *A Study of Thinking*. New York: Science Editions, 1962.

Capra, F. *The Tao of Physics.* New York: Bantam Books, 1977.

Canfield, J.; Hansen, M.V. and Hewitt, L. *The Power of Focus.* Deerfield Beach, FL: Health Communications, 2000.

Carnegie, D. *How to Win Friends and Influence People.* New York: Simon & Schuster, 1936.

Carlson, R. *Don't Sweat the Small Stuff.* Bolton, Ontario: H.B. Fenn & Co., 1997.

Covey, S. R. *The 7 Habits of Highly Effective People.* New York: Simon & Schuster, 1989.

Carroll, L. *Alice's Adventures in Wonderland.* London: Octopus Books, Ltd., 1981.

Dobzhansky, T.H. *Mankind Evolving.* New Haven, CN: Yale University Press, 1962.

Frankl, V. *Man's Search For Meaning.* New York: Pocket Books, 1984.

Fulgham, R. *All I Ever Needed to Know I learned in Kindergarten.* New York: Ballantine Books, 1992.

Gibran, K. *The Prophet.* New York: Alfred A. Knopf, 1978.

Hoff, B. *The Tao of Pooh.* New York: Dutton, 1982.

Johnson, A. *The Power Within.* Provo, UT: Executive Excellence Publishing, 2000.

Johnson, S. *Who Moved My Cheese?* New York: G.P. Putnam's Sons, 1998.

Jung, C.G. *Modern Man in Search of a Soul.* New York: HBJ Books, 1933.

Koestler, A. *The Act of Creation.* New York: The MacMillan Co., 1964.

Kopp, S.B. *If You See a Buddha on The Road, Kill Him!* Palo Alto, CA: Science & Behavior Books, 1972.

Kushner, H.S. *Living a Life That Matters.* New York: AlfredA. Knopf, 2001.

Mandino, O. *The Greatest Secret in the World.* New York: Bantam Books, 1972.

Mitchell, W. *It's Not What Happens to You, It's What You Do About It.* San Francisco: Phoenix Press, 1999.

Montagu, A. *On Being Human.* New York: Hawthorn Books, Inc., 1950.

Ouspensky, P.D. *The Psychology of Man's Possible Evolution.* New York: Vintage Books, 1974.

Pierce, J.C. *The Crack in the Cosmic Egg: Challenging Constructs of the Mind.* New York: Pocket Books, 1971.

Redfield, J. *The Celestine Vision* New York: Warner Books, 1997.

Robins, A. *Unlimited Power.* New York: Simon & Schuster, 1986.

Rohn, J. *The Seasons of Life.* Austin, TX: Discovery Publications, 1981.

Schumacher, E.F. *A Guide For The Perplexed.* New York: Harper & Row, 1977.

Schutz, W. *Profound Simplicity.* San Diego, CA: University Associates, 1982.

Stone, W.C. *Success System That Never Fails.* New York: Simon & Schuster, 1991.

Swift, J. *Gulliver's Travels.* London: Dean & Son, Ltd. (no date).

Szasz, T. *The Second Deadly Sin.* New York: Anchor Press, 1973.

Tice, Lou. *Smart Talk.* Provo, UT: Executive Excellence Publishing, 2001.

Tracy, B. *Success is a Journey.* Provo, UT: Executive Excellence Publishing, 1999.

Vanzant, Iyanla. *In the Meantime.* New York: Simon & Schuster, 1998.

Watts, A.W. *The Book: On the Taboo of Knowing Who You Are* (or any of his other 25+ books). New York: Vantage Books, 1972.

Watzlawick, P.; Beavin, J.H.; and Jackson, D.D. *The Pragmatics of Human Communication.* New York: W.W. Norton & Co., 1967.

Wilber, K. *The Eye of Spirit: An Integral Vision for a World Gone Slightly Mad.* Boston: Shambhala Publications, 1998.

Zukav, G. *The Seat of The Soul.* New York: Simon & Schuster, 1990.

The Book. Wheaton, IL: Tyndale House Publishers, Inc., 1971.

About the Author

The cat and mouse leaders and kittens felt they all needed to say good-bye properly and decided the best way to do that would be to tell the readers a little about their author, Dr. Bill. Of course, they had to have a plan, and as usual it was Khaos who took the lead. She began, "Let's tell the readers all the major things Dr. Bill has done to create his share of chaos and how he has made a few order-restoring contributions. We cats can cover his major life events, and you mice can share what he learned from those events. This will show how his thinking was shaped and how he came up with all the ideas in this book."

"This sounds like a good plan," chimed in Klarity, "After all, Dr. Bill is quite a character."

Khaos began, "Dr. Bill had ADHD before they even had a name for it or Ritalin to help cure it." He always had a nagging inner urge to be great. Everything he did, from playing football weighing only 85 pounds to getting a Ph.D. with an average IQ, were over-achieving efforts to prove himself," remembered Kunfuzion. "Well, despite all that," Klarity said, "It seems that he accomplished a few good things over the years." Simplicity remembered him saying once that ADHD was really not a curse but a gift in disguise. She thought that was a good attitude to have. "He told me that hyperactivity helped him be more sensitive to everything and to hurry up and experience everything so he could learn from those experiences," she revealed.

"Seeing ADHD as a gift rather than a curse just might change the way people look at it," said Klarity. She realized that everyone has greatness inside, but they have to believe in themselves and prove it. "You just can't dream about things like getting famous by writing a book, without working hard to make those dreams happen—and you always have to be willing to make sacrifices," said Klarity.

"Our translator had a fun time growing up in New Jersey," recalled Khaos. "He had two very smart parents who taught him how to psychologize, and he had two neat sisters who taught him all he needed to know about girls. There were beaches, farms, his landscaping business, the neighborhood gang, and all kinds of sports. In High School, he and his friend Al had a contest to see who could date the most girls in their senior year. Dr. Bill was competitive, and he won by a narrow margin, only because Al wanted study harder to get into an ivy league college."

"After the fun high school days, he joined the Air Force and that took him to Japan and Vietnam. That was definitely a re-ordering experience," concluded Khaos.

"After Vietnam," continued Khaos, Dr. Bill, went on a journey to discover truth." "He diligently studied psychology and all the world religions from Sufism to Buddhism. At the same time he was counseling others and being counseled himself in encounter groups for self-awareness and self-actualization.

"So, what re-ordering purpose did this winding journey serve?" asked Kunfuzion.

Klarity replied, "He realized there was a whole different reality out there that couldn't be explained and that all the different paths we invented here all lead to the same place. He learned the importance of the consequences of his wrong choices and that he might have to make a whole new series of right choices to get back to where he wanted to be."

"During his 30-year professional career, our author lived all over the country and even in Australia. He worked at six different careers, from being a prison warden to a human resources director," noted Khaos.

The two mice leaders knew the benefit of these varied experiences, knowing that people, places, and jobs all have things in common but are also different. "The differences are what you try to enjoy and not change." Klarity added, "Wherever you are, you learn to first fit in—and then try to make what you are fitting into better."

Khaos recalled Dr. Bill's biggest career challenge. "He told me that going from public service government work to the business world was an eye-opener," she stated. "In business you have to translate your ideas into action, and if they don't make money then they aren't worth anything."

Simplicity knew there was another more positive lesson, and couldn't resist the urge to say, "Yes, but you also have to be doing the right things in the right way for the right reasons, in order to succeed in business."

"Our translator had all the things a normal person could want but somehow imagined there was more to have," continued Khaos. "He had a great job, lived in a new house in Seattle with a view of Mt. Rainier, drove a new car, had plenty of good friends, was married to a beautiful, smart woman, had a wonderful daughter and even had money in the bank. But he felt his life just wasn't complete."

"By the way," Khaos said, "This was back in 1996 when everybody was addicted to on-line MSN chatting. Of course Dr. Bill joined in the late night sessions and met all kinds of women who wanted to be his true love."

To make a long story short, he chased after what he thought was love and later found out to be just technicolor lust in disguise. He lost everything and ended up jobless, penniless, and homeless. All he had left was his sense of humor and his loving daughter Deisha.

This dismal situation is where Doc found out most about himself. He kind of lost himself to find himself. All the perseverance his father taught him and all the hope his mother gave him eventually paid off. He took blame for where he was and was flexible about what he would do next."

Khaos went on, "He eventually found his true love, Kathy. They both learned they had to improve their own likability and lovability themselves before they could find true love. They both knew the importance of loving people unconditionally, as they were, without trying to change them into what they wanted them to be.

This was all a difficult lesson to learn even for two smart, educated people who were into the second half of their lives. They also learned many other valuable lessons. Actually you just read many of them in this book. Now we can all say good-bye.

Khaos, Kunfuzion,
Klarity, Simplicity,
Chaos, and Clarity

The Real Khaos and Kunfuzion
a.k.a. Simon and Little Mate